Sketches

&

Sketches

&  Songs

music and drama resources
for first-step outreach

MANDY WATSHAM AND
NICKI MATTHEWS

Marshall Pickering
An Imprint of HarperCollins*Publishers*

Marshall Pickering is an Imprint of
HarperCollins*Religious*
part of HarperCollins*Publishers*
77–85 Fulham Palace Road, London W6 8JB
www.christian-publishing.com

First published in Great Britain in 2001 by HarperCollins*Religious*

1 3 5 7 9 10 8 6 4 2

Scripture quotations are taken from the *Holy Bible, New International
Version*, © 1973, 1978, 1984 by International Bible Society. Used by
permission of Hodder & Stoughton Ltd, a member of the Hodder
Headline Plc Group. All rights reserved. 'NIV' is a trademark of
International Bible Society. UK trademark number 1448790.

A catalogue record for this book is available from the British Library.

ISBN 0 551 03268 5

Printed and bound in Great Britain by
Scotprint, Haddington, Scotland

contents

acknowledgements

We could not possibly allow this book to go to print without taking the opportunity to offer our heartfelt thanks to the following wonderful people:

Stuart Pascall for your insight and vision of the role of the local church in this type of evangelism and your valuable input into the first chapter. We are so thankful for your friendship and your great gift of encouragement.

Elaine Brown for your tireless help and encouragement in playing through all the songs, and for being a really special friend and member of the Chrysalis team.

Caroline Watsham for all your administrative support and friendship, and for allowing us to use your experience and expertise from your time at the Birmingham Theatre School and Central School of Speech and Drama for the practical drama chapter. Also for your wonderful sketch. Thanks, Sis!

David Robinson, Tim Goodwright and Peter Laws thanks again for allowing us to use your creative gifts so generously – you are all such talented people.

Judith Watsham for your help, support and encouragement in Wales when our creative juices were running, and for your futuristic sketch – thanks, Mum!

The Chrysalis Arts Trustees Keith Lawson, Stuart Pascall, Katie Flory and Lesley Roberts, for your constant support and encouragement.

The Chrysalis band and tour team Elaine Brown, Pete Flory, Steve Foster, Tam Jones, Stuart Grenyer, Carl Brown, David Robinson, Derek Brown, Gordon O'Neill, Roger Mayor and Simon Wilkinson. Thank you for your friendships, for being great team members and for making all those late night return trips bearable and even fun. We value all of you so much.

Gordon O'Neill, pastor, and the leadership and members of Broadway Baptist Church, Chesham: thanks for your crucial role in the development of Chrysalis and your ongoing support shown constantly in many different ways.

Amy, Jeremy, James, Steve, Kathy, Gina and all at HarperCollins*Religious*. Thanks for all your help and encouragement with this project.

Nick White, for photography.

Terry Waite, for permission to include an adaptation from his book, *Taken on Trust*.

And to our Father God, who gives us life, love, hope, joy and peace, for giving us the vision for Chrysalis and the gifts, friendships and strength to carry it out. We are constantly amazed and privileged. Thank you for continuing to trust us with this wonderful and challenging work.

introduction

OK. So perhaps you're thinking this is just another book on how to 'do' evangelism. Like there's some new magic formula that's been invented, and once you try it then your town or community will realise that they have been heading down the wrong road all these years. Once they have seen the gospel presented in this new and innovative way, it will put them firmly on the right path to walk hand in hand with us as we skip towards salvation! Facetious – yes. Untrue – certainly!

Or perhaps you have bought this book because it is full of sketches and songs that are suitable for use in outreach presentations, from Chrysalis cabaret-style events to seeker services and Alpha suppers. But there is more to it than that. Chrysalis is an evangelistic concept designed to meet people where they are at. It is designed to bridge the gap between church culture and the world's culture, which are becoming more and more different on an almost daily basis of change. When we were prompted with the idea for Chrysalis cabaret events in 1991, we didn't realise quite what we had been charged with. We knew that God had clearly given us this vision to reach people where they were at to break down the barriers and misconceptions that they had about Christianity. We knew there were many people who gave little thought to God and had no notion that he had a perfect plan for them and desired that they know him personally. We knew this to be true because we had been the same.

At different stages in our two lives we had found out the truth about God's plan of salvation and forgiveness and hope, and yet we had had the same preconceived ideas that many others face today. Something needed to be done to turn people's thoughts around and enable them to hear for themselves what the gospel really means, regardless of what other people might have told them or of how it's often portrayed in the media.

What was started in Chesham in 1992 and since then has spread round the country is just one way of reaching people where they are. It's by no means the only way, but it has grown out of the idea that God gave to us, using gifts we knew we had.

In the words of the song, 'Yesterday's News' by Truth:

> *It's time they knew the answer passed down through the ages,*
> *The saviour who brought hope into the world*
> *It's a story of a lifetime, it changes every life*
> *There was a man who heard the call*
> *There was a love that gave its all*
> *There was a hand reached down from heaven to make a way home*
> *There was a cross, a sacrifice*
> *And a tomb that gave us life to last forever*
> *Now my hopes and my tomorrows are with you because of yesterday's news.*

It is yesterday's news, but it is also today's news and tomorrow's news as well. If people don't hear the news, how are they ever going to make a choice to accept or reject it?

> How, then, can they call on the one they have not believed in? And how can they believe in the one of whom they have not heard? And how can they hear without someone preaching to them?   *(Romans 10:14)*

God's vision for us and Chrysalis was aimed to point people to the path where they can find out more. It is designed to break down preconceived ideas and offer people a chance to discover the truth for themselves. Isn't it only fair that people discover that there is a deliverer, security, hope, a refuge, everlasting love, forgiveness, freedom and safety?

In this world that continues to spin further and further away from God, people need to hear the reality of the good news and have the opportunity to accept it for themselves. After all, something this good needs to be shared with people we love and care about. Are you ready to accept the challenge?

PART 1

Background and Rationale

CHAPTER 1

what is the role of the local church in pre-evangelism?

It is not the church of God that has a mission but the God of mission that
has a church.
Tim Dearburn

The church, said someone, is God's only appointed agent for evangelism.

So just what is the church really? Sadly, to most people in today's world it's just an irrelevant building, albeit an attractive piece of historical architecture, visited weekly by people who have little to say to the social masses who live in the shadow of the steeple.

A far cry from the picture painted by prophets and preachers down through the ages, who have always seen 'people' as the heart of God's church and relationships as the key to a new order. Not for them the manic whirl of programmes and activities which we hold so sacred, rarely abandon and often add to! It's interesting to note that two of the major New Testament images of church are images of life and relationships. It's a functioning body of people; it's a bride. The church, after all, is the only organisation that exists for the benefit of its *non*-members.

It stands to reason, then, that if God's church is about people and relationships, relationships must be the key to reaching out beyond ourselves to the twenty-first-century world, which struggles on without God to a pretty bleak future.

In Britain we are all aware of startling statistics that constantly remind us of the falling attendances in our churches. If we believe all that we read in the papers, the Christian church will to be non-existent by the year 2040 unless its headlong decline is halted. Only 1 in 200 people will bother going to a Sunday service, according to projections, while without the funding of the congregations the church buildings will fall into disrepair and decay.

The doom and gloom predictions continue when we look at statistician Peter Brierley's book *Steps to the Future* (2000, Scripture Union, London). He points out that while nearly 1 in 5 of the population attended a Sunday service in 1975, by 1980 that figure had fallen to 1 in 10. In the year 2000 that statistic read 1 in 14, and the forecast suggests that the figure will fall to 2 per cent, or 1 person in 50, attending church by the year 2020. By 2040, Mr Brierley predicts that half a per cent of the population will be churchgoers, leaving orthodox Christianity the religion of the small minority.

Some of these figures do indeed reflect a changing trend. For example, it is no longer the socially 'done thing' to attend church, and the local church is no longer the pivotal point of communities that it was some years ago. But how depressing to read that what was originally designed as an ongoing relationship with the living God, which can bring hope and life to the masses, could be reduced to a minority 'religion' for the odd zealous/fervent nutcase! Thousands and millions of sheep without a shepherd is a very frightening prospect.

It seems today that most people have no idea what goes on behind the doors of their local church. If they have no background in the church, the services and traditions are meaningless. If they have any history of attending Sunday school, it often reveals negative memories rather than positive ones. It's a sad indication of our society that, although 70 per cent of people admit to believing in God and an amazing 90 per cent claim to have had a spiritual experience, they do not check it out against Christianity. On a positive note this means we have not become a less spiritual people, but it's clear people are not expecting to find any kind of fulfilling, deep, life-changing spiritual experience from their local church. Why? How far have we gone off track? Don't forget we are not living in the pre-Christian pagan world for which the New Testament was written, but in a post-Christian pagan world, which makes a very difficult audience.

Of course, we haven't got to where we are, and where we are potentially heading, without a journey. The people who study these things can trace the spiritual climate of the country back to near the beginning of the twentieth century. A number of incidences over the past hundred years shook people's fundamental belief in a supreme being – something every society needs – to the core. One of the most important of these was the Great (or First World) War.

Generations who had been taught by the church that 'God is love' suddenly found themselves faced by the carnage of the battlefields of the Somme, counting the dead in tens of thousands. Very reasonably they asked the question, 'Where is God in all this?' A startling statistic of World War I was that the average lifespan of a second lieutenant was between ten days and two weeks of arriving at the trenches. Where did their mothers think God was when they received the dreaded telegram?

This meant that the influence of the Christian message was diminished considerably, and the process of secularisation continued apace with the arrival of the Second World War and on into the sexual revolution of the 1960s. The church became increasingly marginalised as society became more and more governed by materialism and the concept of 'looking after Number One', rather than by spirituality.

Of course, there were pockets of resistance to this process. In rural areas, the sense of community is still very much alive, with a greater percentage of church attendees as a result. The basis of this church attendance, however, is most likely to be social rather than spiritual. But – is this as bad a thing as we have been led to believe? After all, 'social' is the related word to relationships and life. The real issue is not so much why people are there as what they are offered when they get there! In other words, the question must be asked, 'Has community become the core base of these churches, and has God been squeezed out as a result?' We need people to get out of the 'going to church' culture and into the 'coming to Christ' culture.

Generally, however, these churches are in the minority and, to quote Peter Brierley again, 'the tide is running out'. For the majority of today's society the facts are pretty clear. The church's popularity is waning fast. We are in a decline situation, which all our talk of 'decades of evangelism' and 'renewal' has spectacularly failed to reverse.

The church is often seen as a tarnished shadow of its former self – a fading movie star reminiscent of that heroine of the silent films of the twenties, *Sunset Boulevard*'s Norma Desmond. We remain the harmless relative visited occasionally and seen generally only at weddings and funerals – and even these are becoming few and far between.

So how do we tell good news to a society that has moved so far out of earshot of the church? Perhaps we need to think outside the square, to reinvent church. It seems to us that the early church had it right.

COMMUNITY

First, we must recreate the sense of community that the church is all about. Jesus began with a group, and the church expanded into relationships very rapidly. It was only as the years passed that the relationships and fellowship were replaced by structures and activities. When attendance at activities becomes a mark of our commitment to Christ, then the church is in serious trouble.

Looking at the book of Acts, it is easy to see that this was truly an amazing church. The church that Jesus was describing as his 'bride' was a glorious, vibrant place of spontaneous worship and love in action – a relevant place of community where people experience the living power of Christ in remarkable ways. People must have looked in at the disciples and the new believers who were so filled with the Spirit and thought, 'That looks so good, I want to be part of it.' The attractive-ness and 'pulling power' of a place showing such oneness in Christ is immense.

Do people feel that now? We need to be part of church communities that are so attractive people long to be part of them; where they see love in action, deep-rooted friendships, practical aid to the needy, and a real sense of community. Wouldn't evangelism be much easier if our churches showed this to the world instead of apathy, strife and watered-down fundamentals? It is our charge to present the church as God intended it. The world needs to see us operating well as a team, where God is evidently at work in the hearts and minds of his people. We need to show that there is an advantage to be gained by becoming a part of Christ's 'team' – an upgrade in life rather than a downgrade.

Someone once said that the church expects people to first behave, then believe, and finally belong. In other words, if you Behave like us you will Believe as we do and then you can join our club and Belong. But isn't the role of church to let people Belong, so they can then Believe, with the result that they then Behave? Belong first, be part of the team, then perhaps you will learn to Believe, and will eventually Behave by being transformed to become more like Jesus.

So we need to look for ways of recreating a community of believers. Perhaps we need to reinvent and reinterpret church for our own communities according to where we are situated. Would our service meet people's needs in our particular community if it was on a different day/night of the week other than a Sunday?

We see churches doing this in a variety of ways – for instance, there's the church that started a shoppers' service at 9.30 on Sunday mornings at their local shopping mall. What about a ramblers' service for people who love to go walking at the weekend, or a midweek event for Sunday football players? The list is probably endless. We need to find ways of valuing people more than prayer books and relationships more than Sunday services, and of showing grace more than guilt and exhaustion.

In John 17, Jesus prays for those who will believe in him through the disciples' message: 'that the world may believe that you have sent me … May they be brought to complete unity to let the world know that you sent me and have loved them even as you have loved me' (John 17:21, 23).

FIND YOUR WELL

Remember that church culture today is very different from society's culture. Over the years the two have been stretched further and further apart, to become two different worlds. How many people do you think sing in public together, chant, kneel, share the same cup, talk to people they don't know over a bad cup of coffee? Did you know, for example, that only 0.02 per cent of the population attend organ recitals? None of the above are necessarily bad things, but they are not commonplace in today's societies. We need to work at finding vehicles on which the good news of Jesus can travel, being culturally relevant while remaining doctrinally pure. You'll remember that Jesus himself used a variety of means to reach people – he went to where the people were at and met them on their own ground.

A great illustration of this is his encounter with a Samaritan woman at the well in Sychar, as outlined in John 4. This is a classic encounter between Jesus and someone not even on the fringes of the church. She was an admittedly sinful women who didn't think for one moment that God was interested in her and therefore had no real interest in him. Jesus showed amazing supernatural insight, not only in knowing 'everything [she] ever did' but in meeting her there in the first place. She shouldn't have been at the well – no one went to draw water at the hottest part of the day. Yet here she was, a Samaritan woman, and a rather loose one at that! She had come to the well in the sweltering heat to avoid meeting up with anyone. But Jesus met her there. She would never have gone to him and would certainly have never gone anywhere near the synagogue.

Jesus knew he had to overcome huge barriers to reach into this woman's world. The first was racial: she was a Samaritan and he a Jew, a difference comparable to Muslims and Croats in the Balkans. The second was gender: men and women just did not converse in public, not even man and wife! And the third was positional: she had five husbands and was now 'living in sin'.

As a result of this encounter, the woman brought almost the whole town out to see Jesus. Once they had investigated his claims for themselves, they said, like many others over the centuries: 'We have heard for ourselves and we know that this man really is the Saviour of the world' (John 4:42).

What a result! One encounter at the well, and many others heard the truth.

So then, a drink of water from a Samaritan outcast became an introduction to the good news. In similar ways, the bestowing of a fishing boat became the platform for the calling of disciples, the healing of a little girl was the means by which salvation entered a whole house, and a little boy's lunch became the introduction to a feast for 5,000.

So what are the 'wells' in our day? It might be the local pub or coffee shop, or perhaps local amateur societies, work, college, gym, and so on. If we are to communicate Christ's truth then we need to get out and meet people where they are at. We need to build up real relationships, gain trust, earn respect, and then people may see that Christ is relevant today, still working in the hearts of ordinary people: changing lives, turning people around and giving them renewed hope. If people won't come to the church, then quite simply we have to go to the people.

It is crucial that we identify the wells in our society, keeping in mind the following:

❑ They are not on our patch of sanctified sanctuary.
❑ They are places where society lives.
❑ They provide sustenance and refreshment at a physical level for those who visit them.
❑ They are well known by our society.
❑ They are seen by wise people as an object lesson for communicating a deeper truth.

The Apostle Paul knew this. His particular well, reading from Acts 16–17, was the Areopagus, the council debating centre of Athens. And he immediately latched on to what his co-debaters and hearers knew – that is, that 'there are lots of gods whom you know, but you feel here might be another one whom you don't know' (after Acts 17:23). You'll note that he didn't condemn them for what they did believe: 'all those awful shrines – how could you!' ... not too far from 'all those awful night-clubs, pubs, cigarettes and unmarried couples you spend time with!' What he did was to explain what they were wondering about, deep down, and no doubt despaired of ever knowing.

COMMUNICATE RELEVANTLY

Taking it one step further, Paul also knew that he had to relate to these people in the way he communicated with them.

We read in Acts 17:28 that he used the writings of the Athenians' own secular poets and philosophers to present the gospel. 'For in him we live and move and have our being. As some of your own poets have said, "We are his offspring."'

What a stroke of genius on Paul's part! Those words would have probably jumped out at his audience as being something familiar and comfortable. It's rather like us using an example from *Coronation Street* or *EastEnders*. He used an expression of their popular culture – something they could relate to. In the same way today, we must use the same sentiment. Without talking down to our audience we must find ways to relate to them and speak meaningfully to them. Know the culture you are working in. Know the issues they are up against. Know the music and entertainment that will interest them best. Understand your own local context, but never surrender biblical theology.

When targeting the unchurched, particularly those with no real understanding or interest in the Christian faith, make sure you speak their language.

So what are the morals of the story?

1 Know your society wells.
2 Know how the people think.
3 Understand their cultural setting.
4 Look for the things that grab their interest and imagination.
5 Go to their wells.

6   Don't condemn, but explain.
7   Don't compromise biblical theology.
8   Use their known frameworks of language and philosophy.
9   Think community.
10 Think outside the square!

CHAPTER 2

where does chrysalis fit in?

So we have ascertained that the local church is charged with the task of providing an 'entry point' for people: a place with a sense of community where they can come and feel relaxed and secure, and where they don't feel threatened but can see some of their misconceptions whittled away. It's almost irrelevant where this place is, as long as it is the right place for those people in your town or community. Whatever it is, it must be the first step on what can be a very long spiritual journey. Dante said that we are 'worms destined to be angelic butterflies' – a metamorphosis that doesn't happen overnight. Statistics show that, on average, a person comes to Christ after seven meaningful encounters with the gospel. Obviously, some conversions happen in a big flash of light, like Saul on the road to Damascus, but in the main it is a long slow process.

Chrysalis for us is the first step in this process – a gentle introduction to the Christian faith for those who have little or no understanding of it. It is a place for Christians to invite their non-churched friends, with whom they have taken the time to build relationships – perhaps a preamble to an Alpha course or seeker service in the church. The Engels scale overleaf shows where Chrysalis fits within the spiritual journey.

For you, in your community, this 'entry point' might be something different, such as a dinner-dance, quiz night, football match, and so on – the list is endless – but we have found Chrysalis cabaret/variety shows work very well in

Pre-Evangelism		Evangelism		Nurturing	Discipleship
Chrysalis Cabaret	Chrysalis full length presentation	Seeker Service	Alpha course/ Y2000 course		

-10 -9 | -8 -7 -6 -5 | -4 -3 | -2 -1 | 0 1 2 3 4 5 6 7 8 9 10

No interest...   actively searching/interested   Commitment to a walk with Christ

misconceptions start to go

breaking down barriers and preconceived ideas, and allowing the Holy Spirit to start working.

CHRYSALIS: A BRIEF HISTORY

In the summer of 1991, God gave us a vision to reach our friends and families with the gospel. We knew that they would never willingly walk into a church service – they didn't feel they needed to, it was irrelevant to their lives. This is symptomatic of the marginalisation of the church in today's society. But we knew they needed to hear the truth about Christ, and to see that the Bible had much practical advice and instruction on many different subjects relevant to today. If they wouldn't come to church, then we had to find somewhere that they would come to. We had to find our well.

Our background was the performing arts. We never had trouble filling auditoriums for a secular show, so why not use this incredibly powerful medium to communicate the gospel?

God's vision for us was Chrysalis – a relaxed, cabaret-style show that has been running since 1992. Not in the church, but in the entertainment suite of the local football club, thus presenting the gospel in familiar, relaxed surroundings. Guests sit round tables, have a drink from the licensed bar and enjoy an evening's entertainment. The presentation is a fast-moving cabaret in the style of the old variety shows, using different performing arts such as music, drama, comedy, video, and perhaps – but only perhaps – a short talk or provoking comment or testimony from the Christian perspective.

Over the years we have found many churches who recognise the fact that they need to meet people on their own ground, yet feel overwhelmed by the enormity of the task. To this end, after Chrysalis had been running for three years, the Chrysalis Arts Trust was formed in 1995 to support, encourage and help churches to start up their own Chrysalis-type pre-evangelism/seeker events, and to offer Chrysalis training seminars or workshops on specific aspects of the performing arts.

In addition, the Chrysalis team tours the country with different presentations including live music, video, drama, comedy and testimony. Working with the local church, we provide something the members can confidently invite their 'non-churched' friends to. We usually encourage the church to book a local venue such as a hotel, pub, sports club or perhaps school or village hall – whichever they have identified as being their well for their own particular community. Ideally, they provide a meal and Chrysalis provides the after-dinner cabaret.

This helps church members to be confident that Chrysalis is something they are proud to invite their friends to, and not something they feel guilty asking about. We strive to make our performances every bit as professional as the 'secular' band or show that might have been at the venue the week before. As we've said, we have the greatest message to tell – it deserves the best presentation.

We have been humbled and amazed at how God has used us to break down barriers. Here are some of the comments we've received after organising events around the country:

Your way of spreading the Word sits very comfortably on the shoulders of the modern age.
Doncaster Salvation Army

Absolutely splendid – people are still talking about it.
Mutley Baptist Church, Plymouth

Whole performance was outstanding – the way in which the Christian aspect was introduced at the end was sensitive and helpful.
Queen Edith Chapel, Cambridge

Many have said how they were entertained, inspired and challenged by the presentation.
Cambridge CRN

I am sure it spoke to the staff of the restaurant as well as to the audience who I know loved every minute of it. The young man behind the bar was clapping along with the rest of us during the last song.

Women Worldwide

Please convey our grateful thanks to the whole team for your excellent presentation, 'Millennium Encounters'. The evening was very much appreciated by all. Many non-christians not only enjoyed it but found it very thought-provoking – almost all commented on the quality and excellence of the musical items.   *Gold Hill Baptist Church*

Thank you for your 'Millennium Encounters' presentation. It was an excellent programme and very well performed. It certainly had no 'cringe factor' for those bringing guests, and will help build confidence into people to bring their friends to further presentations we have planned.

St Leonard's, Amersham

These are not arrogant claims for our own achievements, but a demonstration of the power of God when you follow his lead and 'go into all the world and preach the gospel'. We've seen it work. We've seen people arrive at a Chrysalis event sceptical, and leave – not necessarily with redeemed souls – but further along the spiritual journey than if they hadn't come. Scales that have long been covering eyes slowly start to disintegrate. Chrysalis, in conjunction with the local church and its members, can be an instrument in the orchestra that changes irreligious people into fully devoted followers of Christ.

And please note that Chrysalis – or anything similar – won't work in isolation. It must be used in conjunction with a full evangelistic strategy, including friendship evangelism – the Contagious Christian course is an excellent training tool for this – Alpha courses or alternatives, and seeker services. But it is a 'first step' introduction.

Meet people where they're at; gain their trust and friendship; be relevant. Give them a professional and polished presentation, and they'll respect you and your message.

CHAPTER 3

why should we use music and drama?

Art can warm even a chilled and sunless soul to an exalted spiritual experience. Through art we occasionally receive – indistinctly, and albeit briefly –
revelations the likes of which cannot be achieved by rational thought. It's
like the small mirror of legend. You look into it but instead of yourself you
glimpse for a moment the inaccessible ground which seems forever beyond
your reach, and your soul begins to ache.

Alexander Solzhenitsyn, Nobel Lecture on Literature

The above quotation eloquently illustrates the potential power of the arts
unharnessed. If you believe the way to meet the people where they are in
your community is by using the medium of the arts, what do you need to
know before you take the step into Chrysalis territory? This is by no means
a checklist for creating an evangelistic strategy, but rather a few salient
points we have discovered to be crucial for this type of pre-evangelism.
Having learnt them the hard way, we now recognise their vital importance
and value.

IT'S HARD WORK

Be warned! You're entering dangerous ground. Jesus' teachings are hard-hitting, and we need to stand firm and be courageous in our teaching and our witness. When Jesus prayed for his disciples and his people, whom he deeply loved, he said, 'I have given them your word and the world has hated them, for they are not of the world any more than I am of the world' (John 17:14).

Does this suggest that evangelism is easy? It says to us 'hard work', and tells us that if we are to be part of church communities as described in Acts then there seems to be a pain barrier to go through. When you decide to reach out into your community with the Good News you are clearly putting yourself on the front line.

Charles Swindoll, in his book *Three Steps Forward, Two Steps Back* (1998, Nelsonword Publishing, Nashville), says, 'We are all faced with a series of great opportunities brilliantly disguised as impossible situations!'

What may seem at first thought an impossible mission – how on earth do we realistically reach out to people in our community when they have no perception or apparent need for God? – becomes at another look a great and wonderful opportunity to share the hope and love of Jesus to a bunch of people who deserve the opportunity to hear the truth.

Swindoll goes on to say that God specialises in things we think are totally impossible. Being a gentleman, he won't grab them out of your hands if you insist on holding on to them. 'The Lord longs to be gracious to you,' says Isaiah. 'And ... he waits on high to have compassion on you.'

Jesus said in Mark 9:23, 'Everything is possible for him who believes.' What a hope, what a promise! Let's hold on to this fundamental truth as we look at how else we can effectively go about making a difference in our communities.

DO WHAT GOD HAS GIFTED YOU TO DO!

Every believer has gifts that glorify God, edify the church and serve the world. Note the last point – serve the world! Too often gifts are kept within the confines of the church and are not allowed to have an impact in the world around them. We can only be fulfilled by doing what we were designed to do, otherwise we will feel unrewarded and despondent. It is the responsibility of today's church leaders to help people discover their gifts and to give them space to release them and use them correctly. There are some excellent courses available to help church members find their niche, the Network course from Willow Creek being a fine example.

There are times when we are travelling back from a gig in the early hours of the morning on the rain-lashed M1 when it is easy to forget what a privileged position we are in. Especially when the extent of our entertainment is gentle snoring drifting over from the back seat, cramp, and a couple of lads in a Ford Escort XR3i overtaking us while grinning inanely at our tour bus logo (one of our sponsors is an old people's home who let us have the use of their minibus) – and that's not to mention the onerous thought of an hour's worth of unloading the gear from the van at the other end. All this and we are still two hours from home!

It's all perfectly true. But when we think about it, what an honour and a privilege to be involved in proclaiming the greatest message of all time while doing something that we love to do. Knowing that God in his wisdom has chosen us to communicate his message and plan of salvation to people who sometimes have no perception of that hope, is surely the greatest gifting and honour he can bestow on us.

> Then Jesus came to them and said, 'All authority in heaven and earth has been given to me. Therefore go and make disciples of all nations, baptising them in the name of the Father and of the Son and of the Holy Spirit, and teaching them to obey everything I have commanded you. And surely I am with you always, to the very end of the age.' *Matthew 28:18-20*

We are all given different gifts, abilities and talents. There is nothing arrogant about a statement like that: it is just acknowledging that God loves us so much that he wants to give us things that will make us feel useful and that give us a sense of pleasure, purpose and direction. When we trust in his leading and listen to his voice, we gain a sense of worth. Security replaces insecurity when we are given something that we love to do, and this will help to shape our lives and our futures and will positively influence others around us.

God wants us to have an abundant life – 'I have come that they might have life and have it to the full.' He wants us to live our privileged lives to the max, to be happy, and above all to live lives that are glorifying to God. We humans find fulfilment by doing what we are designed to do. We all have a different make-up and design. Different things fulfil different people. Using our God-given abilities to communicate to others that they are loved beyond measure and have an abundant life waiting for them is rewarding in the extreme.

The carpenter loves to create beautiful objects out of wood, the teacher loves to communicate knowledge, the nurse loves to care and make people feel better. When God lovingly created us as special individuals crafted in his own image, he intended us to enjoy what we do. There is a verse in the Bible that says just this. It's found in Luke 12:48 and simply states: 'From everyone who has been given much, much will be demanded; and from the one who has been entrusted with much, much more will be asked.' We have all been given 'much' from our generous, abundant God. Using our God-given talents and abilities to serve should not be viewed as an onerous task. Rather, it's a reward as God works through us, creating a channel for us to do something significant with our lives and the gifts that he has so graciously given us.

This is not to say that it is always going to be a breeze and easy. However much we are gifted and love to do something, every job will have its tough parts (like unloading gear at some unearthly hour!) but the fulfilment, sense of purpose and significance that we can gain from serving while using our gifts is immense. We may be like 'jars of clay' or empty vessels, but if we allow God to work through us and fill us with his Spirit we can become vessels filled with treasure. If we then communicate this treasure through the gifts God gives us, then we are all winning the battle to reclaim this world for Christ.

EXCELLENCE HONOURS GOD AND INSPIRES OTHERS

One of the hardest lessons we've learnt along the Chrysalis journey is the level of expectation from our audience. Chrysalis is about breaking down misconceptions that people have about Christianity, and one of these preconceived ideas is that anything to do with the arts and church must be sub-standard.

The sad thing is that this is generally felt within the church, too. If we had £1 for every time we've heard a church member say to us, 'If only I'd known it was that good, I would have invited my husband/wife/friend, etc.,' we would be extremely wealthy! How horrifying that just because of the negative image the church has in relation to professionalism in the arts and other areas, someone has missed what might be their only chance of hearing the gospel.

Unfortunately, though, those outside the church simply don't expect a high standard of performance when they come to a 'Christian event'. If they expect to be moved at all, it's usually not to either tears or laugher!

We need to turn the tide. If they come to a Chrysalis event expecting the worst, then they need to leave having experienced creativity and excellence.

Performance needs to be polished and professional, with people giving of their best. Excellence doesn't necessarily mean slick, polished and sterile. Excellence means preparation, practice, rehearsal and a Christ-centred attitude. Excellence means confident, gifted actors and singers with words and lines learnt. Regular rehearsals are crucial in building a firm foundation through which God can work. When we make a commitment to solid preparation, not only do we become more technically competent but we can expect to be all the more inspiring and inspired. It is only then that we can enjoy our work without having to forage for words and notes, and allow God to take our best offerings and use them for his glory.

Most important, though, is to use people's gifts correctly and make the best of what God has given. This requires time and work from one person, or a team of people, with the specific role of honing and helping the others to become the best they can. There must be the challenge to move on and take new ground for God.

CLEAR CALL AND CONVICTION

One thing to remember: you can be highly polished and with an obvious gift for what you're doing, but unless you have a conviction that this is what God wants you to be doing, think carefully before getting involved. You must be convinced that you are doing the right thing in the right place at the right time. As we've already said, this work is hard and you need to be prepared to sweat blood to make it work, so make sure you know it's right to be involved, otherwise you'll end up resenting it. You need to be prepared to be committed to the dream or vision for as long as it takes – until God tells you otherwise. And don't forget – when it's done, it's done. Don't carry on with something just because 'we've been doing it this way for years'.

CREATE CLOSE-KNIT TEAMS

If you are going to embark on any kind of evangelistic strategy, it is crucial that you are part of a close team who are not only gifted appropriately, strive for excellence and have a definite call, but who also …

Spark off each other!

Chemistry is crucial to the success of any missionary team in the church. People who can relate to each other actually enjoy working together and like each other. Don't expect great results from a team that is constantly bickering and critical of each other, and who perhaps would not otherwise choose to spend time with each other. This doesn't mean that everyone needs to be the same – in fact, different personalities are very important – but you must be able to work well together. You need team unity, not team uniformity, and you must enjoy spending time with your cohorts. As Philippians 2 states, be 'like-minded, having the same love, being one in spirit and purpose'. Some of the best things we ever do come out of good relationships. We can testify that the friendships we have forged with other members of our Chrysalis team are some of the strongest we have experienced. We love spending time together, and thus even having to lug heavy gear and lose the odd hour of sleep doesn't seem quite so bad!

Offer accountability

Working together gives you the perfect opportunity to forge close relationships and form something of the community we've already mentioned, which is so lacking in the church but crucial if we want to be like the Acts churches. As you get to know each other better then you can be accountable to each other. Ask the question, 'Is our morality matching up to our message?' We need to create a group of loving people who feel able to be truthful with each other and if necessary correct each other, as a loving parent would a child. Remember though, 'Tell the truth in love' – and that really means 'in love'. There has to be a huge element of trust, respect and love in a relationship before too many 'truths' start popping out! On the flip side, of course, you also need to offer mutual building-up and encouragement, appreciation of what your colleagues are doing and who they are.

Show authenticity

We've already said that it is a privilege to be involved in Kingdom building and to be doing it by way of using what we are good at, but with these privileges come certain responsibilities. This means not only living a life that is God-honouring seven days of the week, a life that closes the credibility gap between the things we say we believe and how we behave, but also by taking our giftings seriously and working on them to ensure that they can be utilised fully. Is our desire to be a church-goer one day a week or a disciple who rolls his sleeves up and gets his hands dirty seven days a week? Christianity is not a spectator sport! It's about participating in a team, adding our unique blend to the mix and showing the reality of Christ's love. We often sing in our worship songs that it is a privilege to be called a child of God, and so it is. We need to show that we believe that to be true by discovering our gifts and making the most of them.

PRAY

Having ascertained all of the above, it is glaringly obvious that without prayer our work becomes ineffective. Our weapons – rehearsals, hard work, gifts, invitations to friends, and so on – become like blunt instruments. It is essential to prayerfully prepare for the ministry, for the guests and for each event, as individuals and as a team, to ensure maximum impact.

The reason this perhaps obvious point needs to be clearly stated is that, as we've discovered from past experience, people who are prepared to grind and sweat in this type of work tend to be very busy people with a million demands on their time. It is too easy to run out of time when you are spending hours rehearsing, learning lines, ensuring the publicity and invitations have gone out and remembering to make the place look presentable, not to mention fitting in everyday life and the numerous chores that come with it, the countless people to see, the meetings that have to be attended – and the list could go on and on! Are you out of breath yet?

Corrie ten Boom, in her book *Clippings from My Notebook* (Triangle, 1983) asks, 'Is prayer your steering wheel or your spare tyre?'

She states: 'Prayer is powerful. The devil smiles when we make plans, he laughs when we get busy but he trembles when we pray – especially when we pray together.'

Away with work that hinders prayer,
'Twere best to lay it down,
For prayerless work, however good,
Will fail to win the crown.

It's fun to pray together as a team; it creates unity, harmony and purpose. We need to be passionate pray-ers, entrusting everything to the living God who loves us and cares about what we are doing. By asking for specific things we will receive specific answers. Immerse your events in prayer, and ensure there are others praying for you, too. This is a battleground, and we will not be able to succeed without feeling 'soaked' in prayer, however hard we have worked. God is there 24 hours a day, and is always immediately available wherever we are; whatever we are doing, we need only ask and he is waiting, to listen and to help. Call out to him through the noise of life and allow him to work through what has been prepared. Our inability will meet God's ability, and then miracles can happen.

Allow time to 'be still, and know that I am God' (Psalm 46:10).

So, how to create a relevant pre-evangelistic event using the Chrysalis ethos of meeting people on their own turf?

1 Use your God-given gifts.
2 Strive for excellence at all times.
3 Ensure you and your colleagues have a clear call and passion for the work.
4 Create close team relationships.
5 Pray.
6 Enjoy yourselves!

It's not easy – but it is possible.

CHAPTER 4

how to use music

How many times after listening to a song do you feel in a different frame of mind from before? Inspired, encouraged, motivated, excited, passionate, joyful, charged up, determined, reminiscent, in love – the list could go on and on!

How many people do we see in day-to-day, normal, routine life doing something with a pair of headphones stuck in their ears? On trains, buses, out jogging or walking? We hear it often enough blaring out of car stereo systems. If we ever stopped to think why, it might suggest that music can transport us out of our current mundane situations and take us – however briefly – to somewhere magical. Music has the ability to take people back to different periods in their lives; it can provoke strong memories and emotions; it inspires, creates, feeds and enables people to do wonderful things.

I used to listen to my personal stereo, in the days before I could drive, on the long (and did it feel long!) eight-mile hilly bike ride to work. Probably listening to music through headphones on a push bike wasn't the safest or most sensible thing that I've ever done, but boy, did the journey go quickly! As I listened to different music my heart soared, my spirit was revitalised with new energy, and my limbs joyously responded accordingly.

Why are we so moved or motivated by music? If we believe that all good things are from God – and music is certainly good – then we accept that God inspires musicians and songwriters to write pieces that will communicate a message. Whether that message is about love, injustice or having no bananas, it will be communicated in a creative way.

The key thing to remember about music is that it is simply another form of communication – arguably one of the most powerful forms of communication ever invented.

Melody can cut across barriers caused by language, age, class and creed. A song, as somebody once said, can paint a thousand words.

Music is everywhere. It is used to express emotions at many different occasions in life – weddings, funerals, christenings, football matches, sporting events in general, birthdays, and so on. It can represent different stages and occasions of our lives, both joyful and sad, a clever 'invention' which is a powerful communicative tool.

At some time in our lives we have all listened to songs that have just made the hairs on the back of our neck stand on end. Songs that have cut through all our baggage and spoken straight into our hearts and real-life situations. Tunes that have lifted our spirits and encouraged us to stride onwards and upwards. Sometimes a song can communicate a message in four short minutes in a way a 30-minute sermon, talk, lecture or presentation could never hope to do.

Have you ever been to see *Les Misérables* at the theatre? Perhaps you would agree that it is one of the most moving pieces of musical theatre from recent years, and yet not one word is spoken during the entire three-hour show. If you have seen it, then you will remember the undeniable strength of emotion felt by the whole audience during songs such as 'Bring him home', and particularly during the finale. In fact, the only thing you can see and hear from the audience is the surreptitious dabbing of eyes mixed with the sound of tissues rustling. We're not, of course, in any way advocating that evangelistic events should only use music and never include any talking – we wouldn't want to put all those ministers and speakers out of work! – but use this example to illustrate just how powerfully music can communicate to people.

So then, if music is such a powerful tool, just think about what we, who are inspired by the living God and communicating the message of unconditional love to a world desperate for hope, can communicate. Now we're talking real heart-to-heart communication!

MUSIC – A GOD-GIVEN GIFT

We need to understand and accept this: music is a gift, and, like many other gifts, it comes from God. It doesn't deserve any worship, praise or adulation over any other gift, but we do need to recognise its worth and its incredible power. We must be aware of how it can be used as a key to unlock emotions, to break down barriers and to bring people into an awareness of the living God.

HOW TO USE MUSIC IN A CHRYSALIS CABARET

Variety is the spice of life, to coin a phrase, and Chrysalis cabaret events are generally fast-moving and aim to keep the audience entertained and enthralled at all times. When choosing music, this means trying to include a wide range of styles and types that will appeal to your audience. Generally, there is no 'wrong' music for Chrysalis as long as it doesn't cause your audience to question your standing. Music as part of an evening can be used for two purposes:

Breaking the ice

The purpose of music in this category is primarily to entertain and to create a relaxed atmosphere. There is nothing wrong in performing a song simply for entertainment. If by playing something that they recognise you can make people feel at home and at ease, then the song has its rightful place. If your audience leave having had a great evening's entertainment, then they will be more likely to come back. Isn't that the point?

Secular music to entertain

From the secular music world there is obviously a huge range of music for you to choose from: classical to opera, musical shows to contemporary chart hits, jazz to blues. The beauty of the cabaret style is that you can incorporate a large variety of different musical styles to suit your own strengths and the age of your audience.

Use secular songs to break the ice at the beginning of a programme. Because they are familiar they will put the audience at ease and in a better position to receive something less familiar later on in the evening. In addition, as long as they are performed well, they can be very useful to show that the Christian faith is relevant and not stuck in the Dark Ages! You'll probably find that your audience will not be expecting it, but isn't that a good thing? A typical Chrysalis audience, i.e. those who have little or no understanding of the Christian faith, may have come along with some very particular preconceived ideas about Christianity and what they are expecting to hear: maybe hymns, or a girl with long hair and sandals strumming a guitar and singing 'This Little Light of Mine'! How wonderful to blow away all those misconceptions by starting the evening with a polished jazz version of a Beatles song, or a song from a musical, or perhaps something from the recent charts. You need to be imaginative and adventurous.

Secular music to challenge

It is also possible to use secular songs to illustrate a particular theme and the message of the gospel, sometimes helping people think about the words in a new way. A great example of this is the Celine Dion song 'Call the man', which as far as we are aware was not written from the Christian perspective but which works remarkably well as a challenge to people at the end of an evening. There are many others for you to seek out and find, but one thing we would say is that we are not advocates of changing a few salient words to make them relevant! If the song was well written in the first place, well, don't fix something that ain't broke, as they say!

Challenging hearts

Although entertainment is incredibly important to Chrysalis, once you have the audience 'on your side' and have gained their trust, you can introduce more thought-provoking and challenging music. This can be particularly effective after a talk or testimony, or can conclude a poignant drama sketch.

To worship or not to worship?

One thing you should generally not include at this introductory stage, however, is worship. You must remember that you may be reaching out to those who have very little knowledge of Christianity, let alone an experience of a relationship with the Living God. Worship, therefore, would simply be exclud-ing them from something they are not yet able to participate in. Worse than excluding them, it can alienate people to the point of them not coming back. It's worth remembering, too, that songs written specifically for worship were not originally written as performance material, and inappropriate songs can appear strange and a little bewildering.

Having said all that, there is always an exception to the rule! If you can perform an old hymn or chorus in a new and exciting way – as a performance, not as part of worship – then it can be a very powerful challenge. For exam-ple, by putting old words to a new tune, by changing the time signature, chord structure or key signature, you can put the words in a new light. Some of the words to the old hymns are a fantastic testimony to one person's experience of God, and programmed correctly can add another dimension to the presenta-tion. One example of this is our reworking of 'Great is Thy Faithfulness': old words with a new, more contemporary tune, illustrating the faithfulness of God over times past and into the future. This particular song was placed within a programme after a very moving performance of a monologue based on the experiences of Terry Waite as a hostage in Beirut (found on page 257 of this book). The story of Terry's unwavering faith when faced with adversi-ty coupled with a song depicting God's great faithfulness to us was both moving and challenging. Many's the time we've had people come up to us after a performance of that song with a tear in their eye, to tell us how much it has spoken to them.

However, certain worship songs could be used to great effect at the next stage of the journey, perhaps at a seeker service. There is a definite argument that people nowadays want to actually experience worship of a living God and see and hear the difference he can make in people's lives.

This book
The songs included in this book have all been written with Chrysalis in mind. Written to a broad or specific theme, some are entertaining for a more cabaret approach, and some are more challenging. They are all written from a Christian perspective and designed for use in outreach events.

Seek out contemporary Christian songs
In addition, you will find that there are literally hundreds of wonderful Christian songs available to use, in all kinds of styles. Sheet music is becoming

far more readily available in this country, so look out for Christian artists' songbooks in your local Christian bookshop. If what you want is not immediately available, the shop will probably be able to order it for you, as most will have all the publication lists from the record companies. The world wide web is a great source finder for Christian material, and you can order direct from suppliers and many American Christian bookshops.

Be wary, though – much of the contemporary Christian music available is written with worship in mind, and it is worth remembering what we've already discussed on that subject.

Write your own

If you can't find any appropriate music to illustrate a specific issue, what about creating something yourself? It is often easier to write a song with a specific theme in mind. This is how we started composing when 'the song' we needed for a particular presentation just wasn't to be found. If you do try your hand at composing, our best advice is lean on your own personal experiences. This will cut more ice with the audience. And make sure you run it past someone you trust and respect before it goes on public display. Something you think is a great work of art may not appear so in front of a hundred critical Chrysalisers!

Let me entertain you!

Think of your audience: they are first and foremost coming to be entertained. Believe it or not, they have not left their nice cosy lounges to be made to feel put upon, uncomfortable, embarrassed and awkward.

Any or all of these things are a distinct possibility if a bad performance is given, words are forgotten or praise songs are sung out of context.

Make the most of what you've got

If you are starting from scratch, don't be disheartened if all that is available is one person: music can still be used to great effect. A wealth of material is available that will only require this simple approach, and some of the best and most effective songs have been written and performed by one person on guitar or piano. Once you have ascertained what you've got, you can start planning; work to your strengths and use what you have available to you.

Be bold, adventurous and open. There is no set formula in the programming and using of music in Chrysalis outreach events. A lot of it is down to simple common sense, creativity and discernment. There is very little music that would be inappropriate for a Chrysalis presentation, so whether you have opera singers, a string quartet or a one-man band, they will all be able to use their gifts to break down the barriers and bring people into a greater understanding of why the gospel is relevant for them here and now.

Finally, a point for consideration: if no live music is available, then remember that music can also be inserted in different formats, such as pop videos, CDs and tapes accompanying readings and testimonies, singing to backing tracks, and so on.

POINTS TO REMEMBER

❏ Use music – it's one of the most powerful forms of communication.
❏ Use secular music to entertain and creative a relaxed feel.
❏ Use familiar songs to challenge.
❏ Don't use worship songs out of context.
❏ Entertain your audience.
❏ Use what God has given you to your best ability.

CHAPTER 5

music: putting it into practice

*Putting a band together, vocal technique
and practical exercises*

So now you want to put together some music for a pre-evangelistic cabaret. The majority of this chapter is on developing vocal technique – Mandy wearing her vocal coaching hat with some practical advice for all singers who want to make the most of their God-given gifts. But to start the chapter, here are some basic pointers designed to help if you are thinking of putting together a band for the first time to provide music at your outreach events.

❏ Find a regular rehearsal time that everyone can make. This may sound a little obvious, but it is vital to establish a regular night or time that everyone can commit to from the start and is prepared to make a priority.
❏ Establish the vision of the band – create a mission statement, if you want to call it that. Discuss where each of you sees the band going, what you hope to get out of being in a band, what each person feels they can contribute to the team. Discuss also what styles of music you see yourself playing – this is the point where you may realise that you are barking up different trees, but it is important to set the band's agenda right from the start and to establish some basic guidelines.

❏ Find some PA gear and preferably a good sound engineer to run it for you. The sound technician is the key person for a band, in that he or she controls the overall sound and pulls and mixes the individual components together. Without one, life as a band can be tricky! On occasion, we have mixed the sound from the stage in moments of necessity, but it is virtually impossible to get as good and as balanced a result as you would with an engineer out front.

❏ The first song you rehearse together needs to be something that (a) everyone is familiar with, (b) everyone likes, and primarily (c) is simple and straightforward! In the early days, it will be much easier to put together a cover song that everyone knows – and therefore has an idea of how it should sound – than an original song written by one of the team that no one else knows. Once you have created your 'sound' in the covers and built up some confidence in the band and each other, it will be much easier to work on an original number.

❏ Look at what you have available in the band, and work to those strengths. There is little point trying to perform a Van Halen number that the vocalist has always wanted to sing if the other members of the band consist of two flautists and a conga player.

❏ One person should really take the lead in the band. This doesn't mean that they call the shots when it comes to choosing music, but there really does need to be somebody who can make the final decisions on tempos, cuts and so on, as invariably there will be differences of opinion. There also needs to be someone to take responsibility for distributing music and rehearsal tapes, organising rehearsal venues, ensuring rehearsals start on time with a prayer, structuring the precious rehearsal time you have, and so on. Again, this needs to be established early on and must be respected.

❏ Try to practise individually outside rehearsal time to ensure that time is used most effectively at each group session.

❏ Encourage and appreciate each other. In a band all the individual components are vital in making up the complete sound, and as already discussed that includes the sound engineer. No one is more important than anyone else, and the team will certainly gel better without any rivalry or disparaging comments being muttered. God has graciously 'lent' us these gifts to be used for his glory: we need to appreciate that they are gifts and be good stewards of them in order to use them to the optimum effect.

❏ Finally on this band section, taking lessons in any instrument is strongly recommended if a person shows a natural musical ability. And that leads neatly on to the next section about the voice!

USING YOUR VOICE

The voice is an instrument as much as any other, and it is imperative, if you have been blessed with a natural singing gift, that you learn at least some basic technique in order to maximise your potential and ensure that your voice becomes trustworthy and reliable.

Below I have listed a few of the basics to get you started on the road to a good vocal technique, but I would strongly recommend that if you want to take it further you go and find a good singing teacher for regular coaching. We all have the inbuilt equipment to ensure that our voices last us and serve us well for the rest of our lives, but they will only work and last as they are designed to do if they are treated with care and respect and are well looked after. If a keyboard player damages their instrument in a frenzied moment of playing, they can go and buy another one and sound the same as ever. If a vocalist damages their instrument they can't just go to the shop and pick up another voice from the shelf! This is why the voice is one of the hardest instruments to master: it is so dependent on how we are feeling physically, how we exercise it to develop sound technique, and how we look after it on a day-to-day basis.

Physical warm-up

As with any exercise, it's important to warm up the muscles and the vocal chords before launching into a two-hour concert. Later on in this chapter we will be doing exercise specific to the voice, which will not only enhance it long-term but will also warm it up ready for action. First, though, let's get the entire body nice and relaxed with a few simple exercises.

The upper part of your body, from the waist upwards, needs to be loose and relaxed while singing. The lower part of your body, from the waist downwards, is your workstation and needs to be toned and ready for demands that will be placed upon it while singing.

1   Relax the top part of your body by gently rolling your shoulders forwards ten times, then backwards ten times.
2   Plant feet firmly apart and reach over your head with your right arm towards the left, gently stretching the right side of your torso. Hold for a count of ten and then repeat with your left side.
3   Push your chin downwards on to the top of your chest and gently roll the neck round from centre chest to the left, and then back to centre. Repeat, and then carefully roll to the right and gently return to centre. Repeat.
4   Finally, vigorously and loosely shake arms and then hands from the wrists for about ten seconds. Stop shaking and let your arms and hands drop loosely by your sides. Your hands should feel slightly tingly, and should hang naturally weighted and relaxed by your sides – the perfect position for them while singing.

Stance and posture

Before you begin singing, place feet apart to create a firm foundation. Your spine should be as straight as possible without feeling rigid or uncomfortable. Your chin should be parallel to the floor, with your shoulders square and down but again relaxed, with arms hung loosely by your sides.

Try to imagine that you have a string running up through your spine and out through the top of your head. Your aim is to keep the string pulled taut so that your body will form a nice straight line. Let the string go slack, and your body becomes floppy like a puppet on a string – not a cue for a song!

Try it. You should feel a couple of inches taller, and will look far more like a confident singer ready for action.

This is the best position for singing. Try and preserve the upper body position even if you have to sit at a piano or with a guitar.

The middle part of your body, as mentioned earlier, is your workstation. It needs as much freedom of movement as possible, with no awkward slouching, which will hinder the breathing and in turn the voice.

Breathing

Good breath control is key to good controlled singing, and its importance cannot be overvalued.

When we breathe deeply and learn how to control our breath, we benefit in more ways than just vocally. It can expand chests, build up stomach muscles, re-oxygenate the blood, correct posture and relax us when we are feeling nervous.

When singing, it's important to remember that we all possess two large sacks that can contain air – rather like two balloons – called lungs. In everyday breathing and for things such as walking and talking, we will tend to breathe very shallowly. For singing and sleeping we need to breathe much more deeply. If you watch someone sleeping, you will notice that they tend to breathe more deeply and less frequently. The same needs to happen when we are singing in order to sustain phrases, and in time, once we have built up the relevant muscles, to control the amount of air that escapes through our mouths so that our singing becomes smooth and supported. Our lungs need to be filled with air to the maximum capacity to ensure optimum use.

The diaphragm, which sits dome-shaped below the lungs, supports the two air sacks. When the lungs are full of air it squashes flat, the abdominal muscles below it are pressed down and out, and the ribcage and chest expand. When the lungs empty of air the diaphragm, ribcage and abdominal muscles revert to their original positions. All of this equipment moving in and out helps to support the air in the lungs, and the muscles and diaphragm support and control the rate at which the air escapes. This all adds up to controlled, smooth singing and sustained phrases, with no frenetic wobble to the voice, which happens when too much air rushes out – not to be confused with natural vibrato!

Breathing exercises

The dog
To feel your diaphragm and abdominal muscles working, place your hands on your tummy just below the ribcage, and pant like a dog. You will feel your tummy moving in and out quickly. This also means your diaphragm is moving up and down as well as your abdominal muscles.

The balloon

Make sure you have no air left at all in your lungs by holding your hands on your waist and then strongly blowing all the air out to a pssssshhhhh sound. Your ribcage should collapse and your tummy should pull in tightly. Now imagine you are filling up with air in just the same way that you would inflate a balloon: take a slow, deep breath, filling up from the bottom of your lungs to the top, rather like sucking air through a straw. As you do this, you should feel your ribcage expanding and your hands being pushed out as your tummy expands frontways, backways and sideways. Now slowly let the air out by keeping the mouth almost closed and gently hissing like a snake. Gradually the whole process will be repeated: as the air leaves the lungs so your cavity will deflate and your hands on your waist will go inwards. Keep letting the air out until you feel a tight sensation in your tummy as you pull in to ensure the lungs are empty, and then repeat. Take care not to hyperventilate.

The attack

Sing the vowel sound 'i', pronounced like the capital letter 'I', to arpeggios. As you attack each note pull your tummy muscles in to help the diaphragm's support under the lungs.

Placing the voice forward

The second key to good singing is placing the voice forward: resonance and projection. It is vital to develop resonance in your voice, which will not only aid placing and projection but will also prevent damage to the delicate vocal chords as you avoid singing from the throat.

The exercises below will help you feel your resonators.

Lightly hum

What can you feel? You should be able to feel a light tingling or buzzing on your lips and slightly on your cheeks and forehead.
Practise humming to an E♭ scale up and then down, and feel the buzz!

Next try 'nng'ing

Sing 'nng'. What can you feel? A light pressure in the bridge of your nose? This is a very nasal sound, and while I am not advocating that you sing through your nose it is a great exercise for feeling your resonators in the nasal cavity. (See over for more details on cavities and echo chambers.)

Sing 'nng ooh aaah'

Feel resonators, then from 'nng' sing 'ooh'; from 'ooh' open up the mouth and throat and sing 'aaah'. 'Nng ooh aaah.'

Hum

Another exercise to aid resonance and forward production is to begin with a hum, change to a consonant, then change to a vowel, then end with a consonant. Try this: 'mmm ... ore ... mmm ... eee ... mmm ... aaah ... mmm ... ay ... mmm'.

These are great for preventing vowel sounds slipping back into the throat, a trait that always threatens the English singer!

Rrrrrr

Finally, another great safe way of getting the voice forward is by rolling your 'r's. If you can't roll your 'r's, then try 'brr's with your lips. Sing rapidly up and down an E♭ scale.

Try a similar exercise to the vowels and consonants above, but this time base it on a rolling 'r': 'rrr ... ooo ... rrr ... aaah ... rrr ... ay .... rrr ... eee ... rrr ... aaah ... rrr'.

Creating space in the mouth and using your resonating chambers

The third key thing that aids good singing is creating space in the mouth and using your body's natural echo chambers. Think about an acoustic guitar: the hole is cut from a hollow guitar and the strings are placed over the hole. The strumming action over the hole echoes around the resonance chamber, creating depth of sound and volume.

It's the same with our bodies. We have inbuilt echo chambers, one in the space above our mouth and behind our nose, the other in our mouth, throat and chest space. The vocal chords where the sound is created are fairly weak-sounding by themselves, so the sound is amplified by these echo chambers. It is important, therefore, to create as much space as possible in them.

1 The mouth should be spacious, with a nice loose and relaxed jaw. A good way to practise this is by looking in a mirror and yawning! Yawning is the perfect singing position because it is raising the soft palate and creating

lots of space. The tongue sits nice and flat with the tip of the tongue touching the back of the bottom teeth. The tongue should not rise up at the back and therefore restrict throat space and airflow.

2 Place your fingers behind your ears and drop your jaw. You can feel a hinge, which when dropped creates a lot of space between the back teeth. Remember, the more space you create, the more resonant your voice will sound.

3 Your mouth and jaw should feel open and relaxed. There should not be any aches or rigidity. If you do experience this, practise chewing and moving the jaw from side to side.

Finally, there is nothing worse than listening to a song and not having a clue what it's about. There is no excuse for bad diction, especially when singing songs with a message. And this can be easily rectified by having a few simple rules:

1 Don't roll words into each other, especially those that end on a consonant and start on a vowel: e.g. 'door and' could become 'door rand'. Watch out for vowels next to each other too e.g. 'I am' could become 'Iyam'.

2 Sing the song with the same phrasing that you would use if you were speaking the words, using the punctuation marked. Never breathe in the middle of a word.

3 Use the dynamics marked in the music and if there aren't any, make some up yourself to create light and shade where appropriate. A song needs to be sung with different levels of volume, articulation, tempo etc. to bring it to life and make it interesting.

Well, that's a whistle-stop tour of the first basic steps to good vocal technique. There are many more, but this is not a book just about how to sing, so here we will stop! Have fun!

Try these exercises and see how you get on. Remember, regular practice really is the only way to improve in anything, so try to get into a daily routine.

CHAPTER 6

how to use drama

THE WORLD WE LIVE IN

Drama is a very effective and powerful means of communication. Drama, unlike music, does not have the challenges of preconceived opinions on style and musical content. In fact, drama is usually unbiased and very broad-based, quite often appealing to a wide range of ages and characters.

We live in a constantly improving visual age. Television, cinema, satellite, digital images, the Internet and the advertising media all contribute to increase the expectation of the audience. The movie business is a multi-million-dollar industry. Plays in the West End of London are regularly sold out, with *The Mousetrap* breaking records every year. Our children sit in front of videos instead of reading story books, and the power of imagination is a diminishing capability. As a result, people need to be visually entertained. It must follow, then, that if society's main communication is through the visual arts, drama must and should be used to communicate the truth of the gospel with the same visual impact employed by the media.

THE WORLD YOUR AUDIENCE LIVES IN

On the whole, Chrysalis does not often use biblical sketches; we recommend contemporary drama that reflects the modern world, the world our audience lives in. This identification can make drama a very powerful 'seed-sowing tool', and can open eyes and hearts to the working of the Holy Spirit. Generally then, drama is used within Chrysalis to illustrate or introduce a subject, not to answer questions or provide an alternative to a thought-provoking talk.

You'd be amazed at how many scripts we have seen claiming to be 'cringe-free' and 'written for evangelism' that manage to give a full, unsubtle, gospel presentation in five minutes. They are often full of Christian jargon, raising a point and answering it in a very unconvincing turn-around of events. Perhaps these sketches will work in certain evangelistic events. In our experience, those people typical of a Chrysalis audience – those who are being introduced to Christianity for the first time – do not respond to this in any positive way. In fact, it can often make them feel they are being 'hounded', and undoes a lot of the goodwill created by the friendships, careful programme planning and presentation of the event which have got them there in the first place.

Therefore, drama within the Chrysalis environment needs to be far more subtle. Use it to inject humour, introduce a new direction or raise a sensitive issue for a speaker to pick up on within a talk. Don't try to do everything with a Chrysalis drama – sketches work within a programme, and when chosen and performed correctly are a vital part of the jigsaw.

LESS IS MORE

As we keep saying, variety is the spice of life, and Chrysalis presentations are generally fast-moving and full of choice 'nuggets'. We have therefore found that short, sweet and simple is the best order of the day. If you follow these basic guidelines you won't go far wrong when using drama in a Chrysalis-type event.

Keep it short

In a society that has so much choice of entertainment, to keep your audience with you we have found it best to keep drama short and leave them wanting more. More and more people have digital, cable or satellite TV where ad breaks come every 10 or 15 minutes. The concentration level of generations past, who would happily listen to a play on the radio for two hours, is sadly lacking in today's society.

We have therefore found the optimum length of a Chrysalis drama to be about five minutes. Obviously, monologues will often be shorter and more involved scripts slightly longer, but this would be a sensible timescale to aim for.

Keep it simple

In a fast-moving cabaret show, there isn't much time to load extravagant sets and heaps of props on to the stage – the minimalist approach is far more appropriate. Therefore, little or no staging is preferable. Just a suggestion of a set is all that is needed to create the illusion and make your audience aware of what you are trying to portray. For example, a telephone and letter trays represent an office scene, a teapot and toaster suggest breakfast in the kitchen. Simple lighting changes can also help tremendously. We also try, where possible, to end sketches with the actors leaving the stage as part of the action, as black-outs in cabaret venues are not always possible.

Most sketches used in Chrysalis cabarets need no more than chairs (folding ones are ideal as they take up no storage space at all) and a small table. Make sure, though, when you are using a venue without racked seating, that if the actors are sitting down they are raised sufficiently for the audience to see them.

Bearing in mind the minimal sets, the way props are used can be crucial to conveying a story. All the scripts contained in this book include suggestions for props, but input from actors and actresses playing the characters can make all the difference. Costumes, too, are time-consuming, costly and not always necessary. Again, the suggestion technique can often be the best solution, with actors wearing a hat, jacket or apron, for example, that will depict their character.

Keep it small

As a typical Chrysalis venue is a club, pub, hotel function room and so on, we find the stage area is often rather restricted. It makes sense, therefore, to keep the personnel involved in drama to a minimum. This means not trying to cram ten people on stage for a scene from *Hamlet* when there really is only room for two! We find most of the sketches we use involve one or two characters, with an absolute maximum of six. Some of the most powerful performances we've seen in a Chrysalis event have been monologues or duologues on an otherwise empty stage.

Don't forget, less is often more.

MATERIAL TO USE

This book

This book contains original scripts, written specifically for Chrysalis, loosely grouped under five wide subject headings. All scripts follow our guidelines, and as such use minimal staging, props and costumes. Most use one or two actors and run for a maximum of five or six minutes.

Secular material

Don't be afraid of using secular drama scripts if they suit the subject and programme you are presenting. Many mainstream performers and comedians have scripts published that are not only very good but can be recognised by your audience instantly, making them feel more relaxed and comfortable as it's something they know. Examples include writers such as Victoria Wood, the Two Ronnies or Morecambe and Wise. Having said this, if you do choose to perform someone else's sketch, it must be very, very good indeed, otherwise you'll lose the respect of your audience immediately. Also, don't forget classic pieces – scenes from writers such as Shakespeare or Dickens can be used very effectively if programmed correctly. Just one word of warning: be aware that it is sometimes necessary to gain permission to perform other people's material.

Monologues

Simple to perform and often very powerful, monologues can be used to great effect within a Chrysalis event. Secular pieces from people like Joyce Grenfell and Rob Wilton can often bring back great memories for the audience.

Dramatic reading

A dramatic reading is one of the simplest forms of drama, but if done well can also be one of the most compelling. Used in conjunction with music or perhaps even a video, it can be very powerful indeed. A scene from *The Diary of Anne Frank*, a reading from *The Chronicles of Narnia* or an excerpt from the diary of Terry Waite – all very powerful dramatic readings.

Write your own

It must be said, first, that writing a good sketch is not easy. If it were, there would be more good material available. It is hard to come up with an idea that can keep an audience interested and entertained and that isn't predictable. When you only have five or so minutes in which to perform a drama, it is difficult to tell a story and create characters. Therefore, in order to be authentic, write what you know. When given a subject, you need to relate to your own personal experiences so that the dialogue will ring true with the audience and have a real impact.

But if you are able, writing your own material is ideal, as you can write not only for the specific subject that you are tackling, but also for the actors and actresses that you have available.

Seek out good-quality Christian drama

Although it must be admitted that there are many sketches out there that would not be appropriate for a Chrysalis presentation, there are several books that are.

Willow Creek is a great source of high-quality material. Their sketches are true to the maxim of illustrating a point or introducing the theme without trying to answer anything. However, it must be noted that the sketches are generally written for an American audience and require some simple rewriting and anglicising. Willow Creek have also produced videos of their own teams performing dramas so you can see how they do it themselves.

Saltmine Theatre Company have produced a book of excellent sketches, and although some are more suitable to a church or seeker service, you will find some wonderfully humorous scripts which follow the Chrysalis maxim of short, sweet and simple.

The Riding Lights Theatre Company have also produced a number of drama books over the years, which again provide a range of different subjects and styles.

LEARN FROM THE BEST!

Jesus was one of the greatest storytellers ever. He would tell stories using characters and situations his audience could identify with. He spoke in a language his audience could understand. He connected with people in order to illustrate a truth, and suddenly what he was explaining became clear and alive. He didn't need lots of props and co-stars to communicate; he knew that the message he was conveying was relevant to the people around him, and that in itself was the key.

And don't forget: God gave us this gift of communication, and he expects our very best.

POINTS TO REMEMBER

❏ Use drama – the visual world we live in expects and requires it.
❏ Don't try and 'tell' the audience – illustrate the subject instead.
❏ Keep it short.
❏ Keep it simple.
❏ Keep it small.
❏ Be relevant.
❏ Be professional.
❏ Have fun!
❏ Be God-honouring.

CHAPTER 7

drama: putting it into practice

dramatic technique and practical examples

GORDON: I'm the director here. I'll hand out criticism when it's due and it will be good, sound, constructive criticism and we'll take it in good heart. OK? Good. Right. Now, Bernard, that was rubbish!

Last Tango in Little Grimley, *Flying Duck Productions*

Perhaps more than any other aspect of the performing arts, drama is prone to the 'cringe' factor. *Last Tango in Little Grimley* is one of a number of extremely funny plays all based on the premise that an amateur play will be a catalogue of ineptitude: collapsing scenery, lines forgotten, wooden or ham acting and, of course, the constant clash of egos of the struggling thespians. Although the humour in such plays may have some basis in truth, it is, thankfully, an exaggerated picture. In this chapter we look at some of the classic pitfalls which give amateur theatre a bad name, and suggest ways to avoid them.

Here is a selection of some of my favourite exercises gleaned from various drama schools and audition workshops. These are ones which I have found particularly effective, but you can probably come up with several of your own. In passing, I can recommend the following books for their inspirational yet down-to-earth approach: *Respect for Acting* by Ute Hagen (Macmillan, 1973);

Street Theatre by Alan MacDonald, Steve Stickley and Philip Hawthorn Minstrel (Monarch Publications, 1991); and Michael Green's *The Art of Coarse Acting* (Hutchinson, 1964), a hilarious account of how not to do it!

You may feel your rehearsal time is too short to allow for the 'luxury' of drama exercises and that the time would be best spent going over your sketch(es) a few times. Believe me, it is always worth making time for an exercise or two. The sketches in this book only last a few minutes each. In a half-hour rehearsal it is better to devote ten minutes to exercises, then run the sketch three times and have a notes session, rather than simply run the sketch six times, watching your actors consolidate their mistakes. Apart from helping to improve technique, carefully chosen exercises can crystallise the characters and sequence of events in a sketch, which will make those lines easier to learn.

There now follow descriptions of the exercises and the reasons for using them. Depending upon your choice of sketch, of course, some exercises may be more suitable than others. At the end of the chapter I'll suggest some examples of how you might rehearse a few of the sketches from the book.

BUILDING A TEAM

If I had to sum up the requirements for a good performance in one word, I would say that word was 'teamwork'. Lack of pace, embarrassing pauses when lines are lost, poor use of performance space – these and practically every other fault can be remedied by your actors working as a unit rather than trying to perform as individuals. This applies even if there are only two people in a sketch.

In fact, even if the piece in question is a monologue, your actor can be helped and encouraged in rehearsals by taking part in exercises with the rest of the team. To begin, then, here are some ways of forging a strong dramatic team.

First and foremost, before you do anything else, pray together – and then make sure that you also play together.

Pick a card

Sit in a circle. Everyone takes it in turn to draw a card from a hat. On the cards are instructions such as 'Tell us a joke', 'Describe something embarrassing that happened to you recently', 'Say what is your favourite song, and why', or 'If you could be a famous TV personality, who would you be, and why?' You only need five or six different questions, as it's fun to hear different people's responses to the same question. Give everyone two or three turns – if someone draws the same question twice they may exchange it for another card. This is good for breaking down people's misconceptions about each other (where your team already know each other) or for breaking the ice among newcomers.

Snatch the sock

A more energetic one, this – lots of fun, and it will literally keep people on their toes. Select two opponents and give them a (clean!) sock each to tuck into their waistband so it hangs like a tail. The object of the game is to snatch your opponent's sock before they get their hands on yours. This is good for injecting some fun into rehearsals and getting people moving. You can also use it as an observation exercise for the spectators: for instance, to assess how their team-mates move, their centre of gravity, etc.

Grandmother's footsteps

An old favourite from childhood parties. 'Grandmother' stands at one end of the room, facing the wall. The others make their way towards her from the other end, but if she turns and catches them moving they're 'out'. Good for focus and concentration (two words you'll read again in this chapter). As a director, you can learn a lot about your actors by watching how they move, who breaks out ahead and who hides in the background.

Get (un)knotted

Get your team to huddle together and hold hands – each person holds hands with two others in as random and tangled a way as possible. Everyone must hold hands firmly, so that the whole team are linked. The aim is to undo the knot so that eventually everyone is standing in a circle: the snag, of course, is that you must keep your hands firmly clasped while you 'untie' yourselves. It does work, really! You might like to have one or two members outside the 'knot' to direct proceedings.

USE OF SPACE

I can take any empty space and call it a bare stage. A man can walk across this empty space whilst someone else is watching him, and this is all that is needed for an act of theatre to be engaged.

Peter Brook, The Empty Space, *Penguin, 1968*

So that's it then, is it? Well, it may be that simple to create a piece of theatre, but note Brook's omission of the word 'entertaining' or 'thought-provoking'. There seems to be an unwritten law of physics which states that poor-quality actors will always gravitate towards something resembling a bus queue!

Making connections

Get your team to wander at random round the room – moving in all directions, not just circling round. At your command (perhaps a whistle blow) they have to connect with the nearest person using bodily points of contact (i.e. hands, elbows, heads); they need not necessarily both use the same point. Encourage them to come out with interesting shapes and to use different levels. This should be a quick-fire game – spontaneity is the order of the day. Build up to groups of three and four (if your numbers permit), and finally to a whole-group contact.

It's elemental

Split your team into two groups (or four, if there are a lot of them). Give each team the name of a different element (earth, air, fire or water). Place them in different corners of the room and get them to move and make appropriate noises to suggest their element. Stress that they are creating one unit, not giving individual performances. Start by getting groups to perform one at a time, then combine them – fire and water, for instance, converging on each other with the appropriate resulting sound effects and movement.

This sort of thing may seem a bit fanciful, but it is valuable in freeing up your actors and getting them to experiment with movement in an uninhibited way.

Tableaux

Give your teams the title of a well-known play or film. Alternatively, present them with a short newspaper clipping or a scene from a play. What they have to do is convey the story purely through a static pose. Things to consider here would be: position in relation to each other; eye contact; gesture; and expression. Give them five minutes or so to work something out, then ask each team to present their tableau in turn and see how accurate the others are in guessing what it's about. (If using newspaper clippings, you can allow them to present a sequence of three tableaux to cover the whole story.)

Now get moving

An extension of the tableaux exercises: use the same scenes or stories as for the previous exercise, but this time get teams to extend them into a kind of silent movie. This doesn't mean obvious miming to replace words (flapping of arms to represent a bird, for instance) but working out a sequence of movements to convey what is happening.

With both the above exercises, you can obviously use the actual sketch(es) you intend to rehearse, and it is often valuable to do so. If you have time, though, try and use some different ideas too, to stretch your team.

All this encourages your actors to think about positioning first, rather than words. It is very valuable to have mapped out a scene in terms of arrangement of people on stage, even before the cast have learnt their words. Too often, rehearsals start with noses buried in scripts, and the cast are so intent on learning their lines that movement is an afterthought. If, in the early stages, they can convey the atmosphere and events of a scene physically, it will probably be easier for them to learn their lines as they will already have worked out the feelings and actions behind the words.

So much for getting away from queue formation. The observant reader may point out that one of the sketches in this book is *about* a queue. Indeed it is, and so there is even more of a challenge to make it work theatrically, which brings us to characterisation.

CHARACTERISATION

GORDON: Look Bernard, I'm going to be brutally honest with you. If I'd got the choice between you and Dustin Hoffman you probably wouldn't get the part!

Last Tango in Little Grimley

One theatrical experience that haunts me still is watching a group of adults in a children's pantomime, dressed as rabbits and singing some ditty or other. Their make-up and costumes were good, but their body language screamed 'Get me off this stage!' Now, you may be relieved to note that all the sketches in this book are about people. However, the point I'm trying to make is that, whatever your role, it will only look embarrassing to the audience if *you* are embarrassed. If you are ever called upon to play a rabbit, then don't be Simon, the chartered accountant who knows he looks ridiculous: be Rory, the bounciest, boldest, rollicking, 'rabbityest' rabbit ever to grace the stage!

Here's a fun exercise to break down the embarrassment barrier.

Adverts

Divide your group into small teams of two to four people. Give them each a different but totally mundane product (e.g. washing-up liquid, loo paper, etc.) then send them off to devise the craziest television commercial they can think of. Have you noticed that the more mundane the item, the more wacky and creative the advert tends to be? Who can forget that lady dementedly jiving with her vacuum cleaner while carolling the virtues of a certain carpet freshening powder? You could run this exercise as a competition for the zaniest effort, to encourage them. Remember that everyone must be ten times larger than life – award extra points for use of singing, dance, silly accents or funny walks! If they appear hesitant, remind them of that although we may laugh at the vacuuming woman, the laughter is due to her masterful characterisation, not at her, the actress.

Stanislavski and all that

You've probably heard of the 'method' school of acting pioneered by Stanislavski. To give a very simple summary, this involves deep characterisation – trying to enter the mind of your character so that you instinctively move and speak as they would. The basic way of achieving this is to ask yourself a series of 'who', 'where' and 'why' questions about your character, from the straightforward 'Who am I?' and 'Where am I?' to the more challenging 'What do I want?' and 'What I need to do to get what I want?' Some actors go into great detail, asking themselves questions such as 'What did I have for breakfast?' I wouldn't necessarily go that far (unless perhaps breakfast was two large Scotches and a prawn vindaloo!), but it is worthwhile spending some time thinking about your character, particularly for the more serious sketches. Just reading through and making notes on your character can be a springboard for all sorts of ideas as to how to portray them.

Ute Hagen explains the logic behind this rather more succinctly than I could:

> The total animation of the body is brought about by a correct incorporation of surrounding circumstances, weather, time, character needs, relationship to the things and people that surround me, plus main needs and immediate needs. And so is the animation of the words of the character. They are the messenger of my wishes.
>
> Respect for Acting

Setting it to music

Make up a tape of music extracts. Aim for a wide variety of moods, such as a sober classical piece followed by a raucous pop number, some ballet music, a bit of blues – say about eight different pieces of about 30 seconds each. Ask your actors to think of a short poem or speech they know by heart. Play the tape and get them (all at the same time) to perform the speech, moving and speaking in whatever way the music suggests to them. This opens up opportunities to revitalise set ways of performing well-known pieces of text and can help 'unblock' someone who has problems acting from the neck downwards!

Observation

Without getting a reputation as a stalker, try and observe the people about you – in the street, in the shops, or on television. This is particularly relevant for comedy sketches based on stereotypes, such as 'Mid-Morning with Ken and Jen', which is about television presenters. It is likely that you will be limited in scenery and props, so think how you should sit/look/talk to convey instantly who you are. That said, most sketches will require a little more thought – don't just resort to stereotypical characters but try and 'get inside' your character for a rounded, believable portrayal.

PACE AND TIMING

DAFFYDD: You can't take that long breathing onstage. You want to breathe deeply, you breathe offstage in your own time.
> Alan Ayckbourn, A Chorus of Disapproval, *Faber & Faber, 1986*

So your cast can walk and talk convincingly at the same time, they don't need prompting, they look right. You can relax and look forward to a professional sketch – or can you?

Pace is that special ingredient which, if lacking, really shows up the difference between amateur and professional productions. It doesn't necessarily mean rattling through your lines at breakneck speed, but rather picking up promptly on cues – in other words, keeping the momentum going.

As with singing, timing your breathing is crucial: don't wait until your co-actor has finished his line to take your breath ready to say yours. It may seem nit-picking – breathing doesn't take that long, does it? But if the gap between lines is just a couple of seconds too long, you risk losing the audience's concentration, and once you've lost that you have to work twice as hard to get it back. Of course, I'm not advocating jumping in with your line before the previous speaker has finished. Just don't allow too long a gap. And remember, the gaps always appear longer to the audience than they do to those on stage.

Try these exercises.

Your number's up

Give everyone a number, starting from one. Get them walking briskly round the room in random directions. Each must shout out their number in sequential order, leaving no gaps between numbers. This demands concentration and careful listening for your cue. Once they've got the hang of this, try different orders: odd numbers, then even; counting down instead of up, and any other variations you can think of. You could also get them to run through their lines this way to really keep them on their toes.

Bim bam bom!

A gloriously silly one, devised by a slightly sadistic director! However, try and do this without embarrassment as it underlines the importance of being on the ball and keeping up a rhythm.

All stand in a circle and step from side to side, rather like the 1980s 'round the handbag' style of disco dancing. Clap hands in time, maintaining a constant beat. Oh, and again everyone in the circle has their own number. One person starts a dialogue with another, in time to the beat, which goes something like this:

ALL: With a bim bam boom, and a bim bam BOM *(repeat)*
ACTOR 1: Number three!
ACTOR 3: Who me?
ACTOR 1: Yes, you!
ACTOR 3: Not me!
ACTOR 1: Then who?
ACTOR 3: Number two.
(at which point ACTOR 2 has to jump in, bang on cue, keeping the rhythm going)
ACTOR 2: Who me?
ACTOR 3: Yes, you!
(and so on)

If anyone falters and breaks the rhythm, start again on the 'chorus' – 'With a bim', etc.

A WORD ABOUT FOCUS

Focus, like pace, is something that can get overlooked. The ancient Greeks used the word *metaxis* of their acting technique, to mean 'occupying two worlds at the same time'. In other words, as an actor you should be living and breathing the fiction of the play or sketch, relating to other characters in your character, and so on. At the same time you should be aware of the technical requirements of acting, such as projecting the voice so the audience can hear clearly. This all boils down to focus. There will be hazards in any live performance. For instance, in comedy the audience will respond by laughing (we hope). You should on one level be aware of the laughter and ensure that lines are not lost through being drowned out, but on the other hand you must stay in character – don't be tempted to play up to the audience.

SOME APPROACHES TO DRAMA REHEARSALS

Michael, darling … you do understand there's a storm going on?… And an orchestra of serfs will be playing on the balcony? … And you are a man who's been a friend of the family for fifty years, so you know some of them are deaf? … So you see what I'm getting at, don't you?
No.
I WANT YOU TO SPEAK LOUDER!

The Art of Coarse Acting

A director's task can be rather a thankless one – you may find yourself blamed for a poor performance while your cast get all the credit if it goes well. However, it is essential to have someone not involved in the sketch who can cast a constructively critical eye over things and keep everyone motivated. Here are some thoughts on how to achieve this.

❏ First and foremost, ensure you pray together to get the group focused and feeling like a team.
❏ If you haven't already done so as part of a singing rehearsal, do some warm-up and vocal exercises (as detailed in the chapter on singing technique).
❏ Make sure everyone has a pencil to note down any stage directions.

Let's look at three very different sketches and see how exercises can be used in rehearsal.

'Hurry Sickness'

This one is a potential minefield for slow pace, so start with one of the pace-improving exercises ('Bim bam bom' would be a good one as it will get everyone in the mood for comedy). A lot of the humour is in the contrast between the characters: the busy, angry customer, the ambling shop supervisor, the timid customer and the dense assistant. Although some of the characters are slow in nature, it's important not to be slow in picking up cues.

Start with a quick read-through to familiarise everyone with the sketch. Then get them to put their scripts down. Try the tableaux exercises so they can think about the posture and expression of their character, then get them to move around the room in character, but without speaking. As previously pointed out, this sketch is about a queue, but that doesn't have to mean a boring presentation. Body language is really the key in keeping things moving. Observation is useful, too: the impatient customer (without stealing the scene from the others) could perhaps indicate his anger by hopping from foot to foot and/or humming under his breath – think of John Cleese in *Fawlty Towers* to get the idea!

After you've spent time on physical characterisation, keep everyone on their feet, let them have their scripts back and run through the scene again. Encourage them to keep the movement and body language they have already worked out (although reading from the script may hamper things a little). You may need to stop the action at some points to work out timings – such as Mr Jenkins' entrance. Note to the actor playing Customer 2: have a few words in reserve to tack on to the end of your line 'Come on, Mr Jenkins, where on earth are …', in case he hasn't appeared by the time you've got the words out! The closing lines of Customers 1 and 2 will probably need special attention, too. Obviously, they are each talking to themselves – they're not conducting a dialogue with each other. They therefore need to pace their lines so that their words flow naturally, while allowing space for the other customer to be heard.

Having worked with the scripts a few times, try running the sketch again without speaking, then once more with scripts. As it's a fairly short piece, your cast shouldn't find it too hard to learn, and you can ask them to come to the next rehearsal word perfect.

'Leave Maternity'

Obviously rather more serious subject matter than 'Hurry Sickness'! It is worth mentioning at this point that if you are rehearsing more than one sketch in a session, it is a good idea to take a short break, then do a suitable exercise to change the mood. For a sketch like this, I would advise getting your cast to read through it on their own and ask themselves questions about their character, along the lines of the Stanislavski approach mentioned earlier. The writers have provided useful pointers in the introduction to each sketch, but try reading through the whole thing to pick up extra clues.

To start, then, get your cast to lie in a comfortable position on the floor and close their eyes. Ask them to concentrate on what is around them, working from the wider environment (such as noises from the street outside) to the room they are in, reducing it down so you eventually ask them to blot out everything external and just be aware of themselves. At this point, get them to think about their character: ask who they are, where they are, and so on (but note that no one is required to answer these questions out loud). They should now be 'tuned in' to their characters and thinking of their fellow actors in terms of the other characters, not as their 'real' selves. Ask them to slowly open their eyes and get up.

Again, a read-through is a good way to kick things off. You might get them 'on the floor' from the start, as they should, we hope, be fired up with ideas on their character which should help them move and react instinctively. Although this sketch doesn't appear to allow scope for much energetic movement, there are quite a few props – and these can really help in making the characters believable. Look again at Ute Hagen's quote on p.50, in which she talks about 'relationship to the things ... that surround me'. Maria, for instance, is in her own home, so when she is preparing the coffee she would normally reach automatically for the cups, tray, etc. An actress playing this role would need to think how Maria might handle these objects in her rather distressed state – would she be a on 'auto-pilot', placing the cups on the tray like a robot, or would she betray her distress by (subtly!) making a mistake, forgetting one of the cups and having to open the cupboard again? When things tense up between the couples at the end of the scene, might Gordon be toying with a spoon (which would probably be better quality than the cutlery he has at home) to deflect his embarrassment? These may sound like mundane examples, but even the humblest objects can be triggers for good characterisation.

As ever, keep a careful eye on pace. It will be tempting for the actors to express their feelings in 'dramatic pauses'. This is fair enough if the acting continues through the pause – but too many of them and the audience will be asleep!

You might want to rehearse all Maria and Elaine's sections together, allowing Jon and Gordon to practise together in another room, and vice versa.

After a 'heavy' sketch like this, bring everyone together for a chat about the characters. This should consolidate ideas and maybe even give them fresh ones to bear in mind while learning their lines. A sketch like this needs a lot of thought, so make sure everyone knows their character inside out, and how they relate to the others.

'Goodbye Mr Magnolia'

Finally, a monologue. Obviously much of the work will be down to the actress playing Betty, but the director and the team can still offer valuable assistance.

Betty doesn't need to move much – she can remain on her chair throughout. The interest in the sketch will come from the changing moods as she tells her story. To help her with this, ask her to read through the piece, putting in a mark wherever she finds a change of thought. Many of these changes occur with a change of paragraph, but there are others – I won't suggest them, as it's up to the actress and director to find an interpretation that works for them.

Betty could then try reading the script while walking round the room, changing direction on each new thought. This should put some energy behind the words, which she can retain when she sits down to perform the piece.

The team will come in useful as an audience for Betty to deliver the speech to. Actually, once a sketch is beyond the 'complete beginners' stage, it always helps to have other people watching, to prepare your actors for the real thing. Another way the team could help is to 'hot seat' Betty – that is, to ask her questions about herself which she answers in character.

Finally, Betty could use the 'setting it to music' exercise, perhaps finding two or three of her own pieces of music to reflect the mood of her words.

So there we have it – some pointers and exercises to help you make the best of your God-given talents. Break a leg!

CHAPTER 8

how to do it

Countdown checklist and planner, draft programme and talk tips

This chapter is not intended to be a definitive explanation of how to 'do' a Chrysalis event, but simply a checklist to help you organise an event. We've broken down the planning stages over a year to allow you to plan effectively and to reiterate the fact that Chrysalis doesn't work on its own: it must be part of a long-term evangelistic strategy.

A YEAR BEFORE

Start building relationships

First, remember that Chrysalis only works within the confines of relationships.

Use common interests to build friendships, and don't be afraid of just 'hanging out' and spending time with each other. Go to things that you both/all enjoy, have a laugh together, discover and enjoy mutual likes and maybe even dislikes! Invest time, and once you have built up trust within your friendship you can then invite them to a Chrysalis event. Without the trust and respect your friendship has earned, you cannot expect to receive a positive response to your invitation. Pray for that person on a daily basis, and trust the Holy Spirit to work with you. Don't forget that the way you live your life and what you say and do can be the most effective advertisement for Christianity, and as a song once said, you might be 'the only Jesus they will ever see'. More is said on this subject below under the heading 'Organise evangelism training'.

SIX MONTHS TO A YEAR BEFORE

Choose the date

Which day of the week you choose will depend upon the community in which you live. We have found Sunday night to be a good choice as people don't seem to have too many commitments then, and as long as you finish by 9.30 p.m. it does not cause too much of a problem. However, we have travelled to many churches around the country that choose a Friday or Saturday evening and make it a real night out. If you are planning a meal with after-dinner cabaret, Friday or Saturday nights are really the ideal evenings to host your event.

The time of year may also make a difference if you want to use a particular theme such as Valentine's Day, Easter or Christmas.

Book the venue

As outlined in earlier chapters, the importance of meeting people on their own ground includes where you choose to hold the event. Have a look at what's around in your local community and look for somewhere people attend on a regular basis. How about the local sports club or a hotel function room? Many pubs often have separate function rooms, and some school halls can be made appropriate with the right lighting and *je ne sais quoi* to create atmosphere! You can often find that these venues are rarely used on Sunday evenings and can therefore be hired at very reasonable rates. Please note: make sure you confirm all bookings in writing.

Organise evangelism training

It is crucial that your church membership understands that Chrysalis does not work in isolation. The success of the evening is dependent upon Christians forging good sincere relationships with those outside the remit of the church and gaining enough trust to be able to invite them to an event such as this. Indeed, it depends on Christians forming the type of friendships that make people actually want to go with them to a night out at the cabaret! It is not simply a question of peering over the garden fence, introducing yourself and then: 'By the way – what are you doing on Saturday evening?'

So, first, leaders must have the responsibility of encouraging folk to widen their circle of friends. Sadly, it seems that the longer someone has been a Christian the less effective they will be, simply because most of their friends are already Christians; as American evangelist Dan Owens once said during a challenging talk on friendship evangelism, 'Sometimes it sure seems easier and more fun hanging out with other lamps!' We do need to start breaking out of the church cocoon and getting out into the world to make a real difference for Christ – not just to ram the Bible down their throats and get our membership numbers increased, but to show them the life-changing love of Jesus.

Following on, there are many excellent resources available to train people in building these relationships and sharing their faith, including the 'Contagious Christian' course from Willow Creek Resources and 'Friendship Evangelism Training' by the Luis Palau Organisation, to name but two.

Let us tell you, there is nothing more encouraging and inspiring than playing a part in the process that changes someone's life. All the teaching and sermons in the world cannot beat that feeling that you have played a part in making a difference. Not only does it change someone else's eternity, but it refuels your own fire and brings you closer to God.

Organise follow-up events

In the same way that pre-event training is crucial, so too is the follow-up. It is therefore essential that you programme this into your diary now – perhaps another cabaret event two months later, or a special seeker service, or even an Alpha course.

We cannot reiterate enough the importance of follow-up and a full, prayerfully planned and thought-out evangelism strategy, otherwise the seeds sown at your Chrysalis event will simply be like those that land on the rocky ground, which take root but are then strangled, wither and die. You need to keep the momentum going and ensure that you have thought and planned the next event so that this information is available to people attending your Chrysalis-style presentation. If they have been challenged and are ready to go along to something else, it's a lot easier to invite them then and there, while they are still thinking through what they have heard. Chrysalis is just the first step in a spiritual journey; to reiterate a point from an earlier chapter, statistics tell us that on average most people have seven 'meaningful encounters' with the gospel before they are ready to make a commitment.

SIX MONTHS BEFORE

Priority prayer

Ensure your church is praying both for the event and for the people they are planning to invite. Don't forget that the Holy Spirit is working behind the scenes in ways we cannot see; it is vital to pray that people respond to his promptings. Never underestimate the unseen power of the Holy Spirit.

Choose your subject and programme

Decide what particular subject you intend to tackle and then start building a programme around that theme. Remember that variety is the spice of life, so keep the programme entertaining and use as many different media as possible. Choose music and drama to entertain, and include a short talk to focus the subject from the biblical perspective. Don't go overboard, though – remember that Chrysalis is pre-evangelism. The idea is purely to break down barriers and misconceptions, so bear in mind the following when putting together the 'talk'. These are some thoughts from Rev. Gordon O'Neill, a regular Chrysalis speaker:

❏ For an average church member, good preaching begins in the Bible and then builds bridges from the Bible to real-life situations. For a Chrysalis audience, the reverse is probably what works best – to begin in their world, connecting to their needs, showing that you understand where they are. When you have established that, you can show them the relevance of the Bible to those situations. In a sense, you are building a bridge from their world to the world of Scripture. To do this, you need to understand their language and culture. Your talk should be biblically based but not biblically confined.

❏ It is vital that you keep focused on the question 'With whom am I communicating?' Even though you can probably assume a large proportion of your audience are Christians, do not try and operate a double agenda. Apart from anything else, these Christians have probably bought their friends to the event in the hope that you can address needs and questions they don't feel confident dealing with – don't let them down.

❏ Assume a basic ignorance of Scripture, and if you want to quote from Scripture keep it short and simple. Invariably, you will only want to quote a verse or two, with a brief explanation.

❏ An example is more powerful than an explanation, so use well-chosen illustrations and quotes which can often take the place of a lengthy exposition. These illustrations and quotes can come from all kinds of places, and as a communicator cast your net as widely as possible. Radio, TV, newspapers, magazines and life in general are all a rich source of stories. For example, Shakespeare may have been the Man of the Millennium, but most people do not inhabit the world of Hamlet. The world of soap opera, however – well, that's a different kettle of fish. Few people would admit to watching them but many people do, and at any given time one of the soaps will be running a high-profile story that even those who genuinely do not watch them are aware of. This can be a great point of contact with your audience.

❏ Humour can be a great way to break down barriers quickly and set people at ease, but it can also fall flat. So make sure you know your own limitations, and if you can't tell a joke – don't try!

❏ Have confidence in God. You cannot talk someone into the Kingdom of God. The nature of Chrysalis means that you should not be making an appeal as part of your talk. You need to have the confidence to allow the Holy Spirit to go on working long after you have finished speaking.

❏ Be specific about what you want people do to – perhaps you have a book you would like to recommend or a leaflet you'd like them to take. Suggest that, if they have questions, they may like to talk with whoever they came with or with a member of the team. You may want to invite them to an enquirers course. Whatever it is, it's a question of giving them an opportunity and allowing them to make the decision. Never try and pressurise people into doing something they do not want to do – give them an opportunity, not an ultimatum.

When putting your programme together, the hope and prayer is that the material will fuel conversations that carry on after the presentation has long finished, and will encourage people to come again to find out more. Here are some salient points to remember as you programme:

1   Try and get the audience's attention in the first five minutes, perhaps by using an eye-catching video or a well-known song – this also helps to create a relaxed atmosphere.
2   Don't forget you're putting together a show for an audience, not a service for a congregation – there is a distinct difference – so don't expect audience participation.
3   Avoid 'church-speak' or 'Christian jokes'.
4   An hour and ten minutes is about the maximum length of a programme. Anything longer than that, include a interval. This is particularly appropriate if there is a bar or refreshments. Remember the maxim 'less is more', and leave the audience wanting more.
5   Keep the age and type of your audience in mind and choose appropriate material. When pertinent, obtain the necessary permission to perform songs or sketches (you are free to use those written for this book).

Here is a sample Chrysalis programme. It is based on the theme of love and relationships, and is ideally suited to an after-dinner environment.

Song	*West Side Story* medley	Bernstein	9.00
Welcome			9.06
Song	'Tell Him'	Streisand/Dion	9.08
Video	*Four Weddings and a Funeral*		9.12
Drama	'Do I Look Fat in This?'	Matthews	9.14
Song	'Can't Buy Me Love'	The Beatles	9.19
Testimony	(about difference between men and women)	9.23	
Song	'Opposites Attract'	Watsham	9.28
Video	*An Officer and a Gentleman*		9.32
Drama	'Goodbye Mr Magnolia'	Watsham	9.34
Song	'My Heart Will Go On', including *Titanic* video	Celine Dion	9.39
Talk	(including sacrificial love)		9.43
Song	'Give It Away'	Soulmates	9.50
Close			9.55
Song	'Love of Another Kind'	Amy Grant	9.57

THREE MONTHS BEFORE

Start rehearsals

It is essential that you allow enough time for rehearsal. Both music and drama teams must rehearse regularly to ensure a polished performance. In addition, we recommend that you allow time for a full run-through of the whole event, including any video or readings, to make sure the programme runs smoothly and to allow any hitches to happen then rather than during the performance! If you are booking an outside venue, this will probably have to be done on the day.

Organise prayer groups

You will find that there will be some members of your church who, for some reason or another, do not feel Chrysalis is an appropriate venue for them to invite their friends to. However, they can support you in prayer, so ask these people to set up a prayer group to pray specifically on the day for everything that's going on. Give them a full list of those involved, the programme and any specific prayer requests, including the names of invited guests.

Organise the meal (if you are including dinner)

Chrysalis works particularly well as an after-dinner cabaret. This obviously requires a great deal of work, and if you are going down this road you need to plan the menu in advance. Choose something that is simple to prepare and serve, but tasty and attractive – something like a pasta dish with a fresh salad on each table works well, or a finger buffet, perhaps. But do try to avoid quiche and salad! There is, of course, nothing wrong with quiche – it's just that it seems to be provided at almost every single church event we've ever been to, and is rarely served at any other event outside the Christian church! Bear in mind what would be served in the local pub, and work on that basis. If appropriate, you might like to think about serving wine with the meal, and coffee and mints afterwards. At this stage we would like to point out that we are not saying that every outreach event of this nature needs alcohol. We are aware of mixed feelings on this subject, but remember that in this country pubs are very much part of our communities and culture and therefore part of life. You will need to address this issue depending on your community and the people you are trying to reach.

We would suggest starting the programme once the plates have been cleared but while people are still enjoying their coffee.

One particular event we were booked for sticks in our minds as ideal. The venue was the local rugby club, guests were served a three-course meal with wine from the bar, and we were booked as the after-dinner cabaret. Eighty per cent of the audience that night never attended church, and they thoroughly enjoyed the whole evening. Live entertainment these days seems to be rare, and many people said how much they appreciated the chance to go out for a good meal, good wine and good entertainment for only £10 per head. The church reported later that many barriers and misconceptions had been broken that night.

Encouragement of church members

Make sure your church leadership reminds the church members on a regular basis of the opportunity that this type of event offers them. Unfortunately we all need to be reminded of the importance of introducing people to the gospel, and the church will take the lead from those in the pulpit.

ONE MONTH BEFORE

Prepare and make available invitation cards

It is relatively easy and cheap to prepare invitation cards for your church members to give to their friends. It often makes more of an impact if the guest has been given a card rather than just a verbal invitation. Make sure the cards include the date, time, place and any other relevant information, such as any special guests or if there is a bar. We would also suggest that you include the words 'sponsored by ...' and your church name, to give the event authenticity.

You also need to decide whether or not to charge for the event, and here we know the church is fairly equally split. While we agree with the feeling that we can't really charge for sharing the Good News, by making a small charge you are, first, gaining commitment from that person, and second, showing that the evening is worth something. Unfortunately, if something is free the implication can be that it is substandard. Obviously, if you are providing a meal or refreshments it is much easier to charge a price based on that. Out of the hundreds of events we have been invited to attend, some have been charged for and some not. We've yet to see any difference in the effectiveness of either, so make your decision based on your community and your potential audience.

Print and send out posters and publicity

Although Chrysalis works on the basis of friendship evangelism and hence invited guests, there is no harm in publicising the event so that when someone is invited they will perhaps have already seen a poster or an article in the local paper. Posters need to be clear and eye-catching and should include place, date, time and any other relevant information. Don't make it too wordy – it needs to catch people's eye as they drive past.

Send out press releases

Do some research and find out the names and contact details of all your local papers and radio stations. Write a simple press release including all details, and try to find an angle that will be of interest to the papers and radio. Make sure it is typed in double spacing and type the word 'ends' at the end! It is very important that the press release lands on the desk of the right person, as they receive hundreds of articles each week from organisations wanting free publicity.

Organise table and room decorations

The first thing we would recommend is that the room is not set out in rows, auditorium-style. It is better to have tables and chairs to create a more relaxed atmosphere, and small tables are better than large ones. Remember that people usually come to a Chrysalis in twos or fours, and prefer to sit with people they know rather than join a long trestle table of strangers.

It is very important to create a welcoming and attractive environment for your guests, and the room decor can be vital to this. Perhaps you can choose decorations to go with your theme – red roses on the tables for a Valentine dinner, for example. Simple touches can make all the difference, so look out for people who have creative gifts and give them the responsibility for making the room attractive.

Lighting is also helpful in creating a relaxed atmosphere, so try and organise lamps or even candles rather than bright overhead fluorescents, which can make it very difficult to feel inconspicuous. And one of the most crucial ingredients is background music. Make sure you have plenty of tapes or CDs ready for before, after and during the interval of the presentations. Don't choose a praise or worship tape, though – something in keeping with the evening would be appropriate.

Organise refreshments if necessary

If you are not providing a meal, your guests will probably expect some sort of refreshments. So, if your venue doesn't have a bar, make sure you have bought refreshments to provide for your guests. Again, these could suit the theme: a glass of fruit punch for a summer event or mulled wine for a Christmas event, perhaps. Whichever you choose, it's a nice touch to provide some sort of 'nibbles' on the tables – crisps or peanuts, for example.

TWO WEEKS BEFORE

Visit the venue to agree stage and layout

If you are using a venue you are not familiar with, it makes sense to visit to make sure there is room for all the people involved, and to decide where you are putting your screen if you are using video and suchlike. It all makes sure you don't waste too much time on the day.

Print programmes

Once the timetable is finalised, put together a simple programme to have available on the tables for your guests. Not only does this outline what the items are and who's involved, it's also an ideal place to list other events coming up, such as special services and follow-up courses – and, of course, the next Chrysalis.

So we hope you've found our 'Chrysalis checklist' helpful. Bear in mind that different cultures and communities have different needs: use the basic

Chrysalis skeleton and build appropriate presentations and events around that.

Don't forget the aim of Chrysalis – to meet people where they're at. So go for it! You'll see seeds sown and people take another step along the journey, and you'll have a great time doing it!

PART 2

Sketches and Songs

love and marriage go together like what?

Love and relationships

This section contains four songs and five sketches based loosely around the subject of love and marriage.

It encompasses different types of love including friendship, motherly love and romantic love, plus some comic looks at relationships.

If you are basing your cabaret or service around this ever-popular subject, you should find something to fit the bill here.

SONGS

- ❏ Friends for Life
- ❏ Real Life
- ❏ Opposites Attract?
- ❏ New Beginnings

SCRIPTS

Do I Look Fat in This?

A light-hearted look at how communication can break down in relationships, and how men and women seemingly speak totally different languages.

Goodbye Mr Magnolia

One woman's account of the breakdown of her marriage and how she is adjusting to her new circumstances. A poignant but humorous message of survival.

Listen with Mother

A conversation between a middle-aged daughter and her deaf mother, neither of whom seems to be particularly interested in the other's life.

Mid-Morning with Ken and Jen

A skit on daytime TV, encompassing a phone-in on relationships and showing an obvious lack of communication between Ken and Jen.

Good to Talk

An illustration of how we forget to communicate with the people we think we know best. The sketch is set in a pub.

Friends for Life

Words and music by Mandy Watsham

For Nicki, a truly God-given friend and soulmate,
and for all other precious friends and friendships.

This song is all about friends – the type of special friendships that enhance our lives, and that you really feel are part of God's amazing creation plan in giving something so special for free and gratis!

It is a ballad which works really well when sung as a duet – any combination of either sex works equally well. The song can be split into two parts where you see fit or feel is appropriate. For example, you may want to sing a whole verse each or you may want to split the verse into sections and sing appropriate lines. The chorus ideally needs to be sung by both people in unison, or preferably in harmony. Likewise, the bridge really works when split into sections, with Voice 1 singing the first two lines, Voice 2 singing the next two lines, and both voices singing the last two lines. At this point harmony works very well, with some ad libs if possible: this is where the song reaches its crescendo as it goes into the final chorus. The reason we haven't written specific harmonies is that it very much depends on what combination of males/females are singing the song.

The words focus mainly on human friendship and agape love, but in the bridge they start to refer to Jesus as the 'ultimate of friends' whose love is seen living through our God-given friendships.

The piece finishes with the final note – 'always' – sustained over some 'crunchy' chords, eventually resolving to the key chord.

Friends for Life

Verse 1
There's moments in lifetimes
when special friends appear,
those you can count on till the end.
And in that instant
when hearts combine as one,
you know God's blessed you once again.
Ever since dawn of time we were planned as friends,
unfailing love, committed to the end.
So when in our lifetimes
we find these precious jewels,
cherish the treasure, give without fear.

Chorus
Friends for life, that's how it's gonna be,
knit together, bearing pain and pleasure.
Got to be, created on one page
friends for life, forever and always.

Verse 2
Sharing one wavelength,
pooling hopes and dreams and plans,
soaring on the wings of song.
Finishing phrases, knowing what you're going to say,
seeing the best in times of wrong.
From heart to heart and mind to mind are we.
Pretence stripped away, trust brings reality.
This friendship's amazing,
God knows our every need.
He gives this miracle for free.

Chorus

Bridge
This covenant of love will live for all eternity,
A rainbow in the grey skies and the blue.
The ultimate of friends was sacrificed upon a tree,
And I know his love is true.

I see him live in you.
And I know I've found my friend for life in you,
   you.

Chorus

Friends for life,
Forever and always.

Real Life

Words and music by Mandy Watsham

For 'Gilly'

This song is a ballad based on the theme of loss. It was actually written following bereavement, but many people have said how they have identified with it after the break-up of a relationship as well.

The song talks about how real life can sometimes really hurt, and how the bereaved person is longing for the long night to end and the sunrise to dawn on a new day, in the vain hope that pain will seem to be less acute in the morning: 'and the chilling nights can sometimes feel so long I need to just believe that sunrise will soon dawn'.

The chorus has the refrain: 'Guess this is real life with all its highs and lows. I'm living real life, here's one more thing to show that living real life can sometimes hurt so bad, but I've got to live real life till I'm home.'

It's not all doom and gloom, though. After an eight-bar instrumental break, the song finishes with the coda, which talks about a place where pain has never been, where the cool scent of morning dawns eternally. The subtle message of hope is that perhaps this particular place is really 'real life' and that whatever has parted us in this life need not part us for eternity.

Real Life

Ly - ing in my bed can't stop the dream-ing,_____ the

slight-est sound will wake me from_ my_____ sleep._____ And the

face I see_ that haunts each me-mo - ry_____ is yours,_____ smil-ing

up at me_ so_____ lov - ing - ly, is yours._____ The

sounds I hear so clear in-side my_____ head,_____ the

sweet-est voice that soothed time and a - gain._____ And this

ache that's formed is here be - cause you've gone,_____ ne - ver

could be - lieve_ that pain could feel so strong._____ Guess

Lying in my bed can't stop the dreaming,
the slightest sound will wake me from my sleep.
And the face I see that haunts each memory is yours,
smiling up at me so lovingly, is yours.
The sounds I hear so clear inside my head,
the sweetest voice that soothed time and again.
And this ache that's formed is here because you've gone,
never could believe that pain could feel so strong.

Chorus
Guess this is real life with all its highs and lows.
I'm living real life, here's one more thing to show
that living real life can sometimes hurt so bad,
but I've got to live real life till I'm home.

Swollen eyes that ache from all their crying,
the heavy weight of sorrow pressing down.
And the chilling nights can sometimes feel so long,
need to just believe that sunrise will soon dawn.

Chorus

(Instrumental for 8 bars)

Coda
Once upon a dream, a perfect land where pain's not been.
Here is real life, this dream is real life.
The bright rays of morning, the cool scent of morning,
someday the morning will dawn eternally,
And on that morning we're home at last and free.

Opposites Attract?

Words and music by Mandy Watsham

For ... one of my closest friends!?

This piece is really a cross between a song and a drama sketch, so we've called it a musical drama!

The main theme of the piece is to highlight the difference between men and women and how they think and behave, and the trouble that this can sometimes cause in basic communication.

It is rather obviously designed to be sung by a man and a woman. The playing age of the couple can be anything from twenty-something to middle-aged. There are sections of the piece that are sung and sections that are spoken, and where there is dialogue a basic piano vamp needs to be played underneath the actors' lines; examples of this appear in the keyboard part.

The piano has three basic styles for the different sections: vamp, arpeggio and chordal. This is to help convey the drama and mood of each different section of the piece.

This is a comedy number and requires a lot of characterisation from the two actors – not too difficult, as most of us can base at least some of it on real-life experience! Sufficient dialogue is written into the piece, but if the couple singing this are able there is plenty of room for ad-libbing and additional dialogue.

It may be helpful when performing this number to think of songs such as 'I Remember It Well' from *Gigi* and 'Anything You Can Do I Can Do Better' from *Annie Get Your Gun*, to convey the mood, humour and style of the piece. Have fun!

Opposites Attract?

I in-formed you I would be la - ter,__ be-cause I was go - ing to the__ the-a - tre.

(It was really good, thanks for asking.) MAN: That's not a thing I can re-call. I
(looks genuinely puzzled)

(etc.)

don't think it was me you spoke__ to. You prob-ab - ly told__ your

friend Max-ine,__ as she gets told life's de-tails to the ut - most de - gree!

WOMAN: I on-ly phoned to let her know I'd

(etc.)

booked her a tick - et for the show. I can't be - lieve we can talk at length, and

you have no re - col - lec - tion, hence it goes to show what I've known all a-long: you

| F | G | C | F | G | C | 4/4 |

choose to be deaf when it suits you so. He choos-es to be deaf when it suits him so.

♩ = 126

CHORUS:

F

WOMAN: Why are men so an-

(etc.)

| C7 | F | Dm | F | G | C |

-noy-ing-ly deaf? When it comes to con-ver-sa-tion I'm just wast-ing my breath. They ac-

| Bb | Gm | C | Dm |

-cuse you of pratt-ling on and chat-ting at length, then they'll

| G | G7 | Dm | G | C | F |

hear the things they want to hear and dis-re-gard the rest. WOMAN: Why are men so in-
MAN: (Pardon?)

(etc.)

| C7 | F | Dm | F | G | C |

-cre-di-bly slow to pick up on our sig-nals that we bla-tant-ly show? There are

| Bb | Gm | C | Dm |

times I need a hug and some e-mo-tion-al dra - ma,___ but the

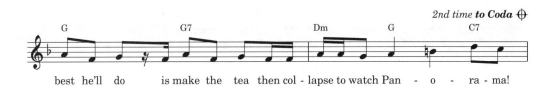

2nd time **to Coda** ⊕

best he'll do   is make the tea then col-lapse to watch Pan - o - ra-ma!

Why oh   why can't you be more like me?_   We'd real-ly get a - long___

fa - mous-ly._____   WOMAN: Ohhhh! MAN: Now lis-ten ve-ry care-ful-ly, here's
MAN: (Aren't we over-reacting slightly?)

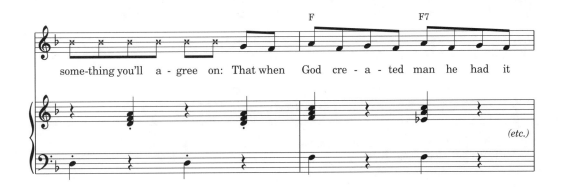

some-thing you'll a - gree on: That when God cre - a - ted man he had it

(etc.)

all with-in his plan to cre - ate a spe-ci - a - li - ty, full of charm-ing fe - mi - ni - ty.—

F (vamp on F under dialogue)   *D.§ al Coda*

(Dialogue) Good we can laugh about our differences, isn't it? . . .

CODA

(MAN:) Why   oh   why   can't you   be more like me?_   We'd real-ly get a - long_

(etc.)

fa - mous-ly._____

(He grins hopefully at her, she is not amused
– ad lib if appropriate)

MAN: Just as

WOMAN: life would be   real - ly ra - ther tame.

well we're not the same.   MAN: If   by

(etc.)

WOMAN: I know I can   al - ways count on you.

chance I'm feel - ing blue.   MAN: This I'll

WOMAN: you are   still my cup of   tea.   WOMAN: Cup of
state quite hon - est - ly.   MAN: (Two sugars, thanks.)

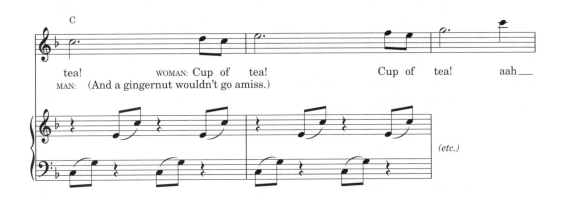

tea!   WOMAN: Cup of   tea!   Cup of   tea!   aah___
MAN: (And a gingernut wouldn't go amiss.)

(etc.)

Maestoso

BOTH: And af - ter
(show off)

all   is   said and   done_____   you're   still   my   num - ber

one!_____

(Vamp on C then B/C)

WOMAN: Hello, love, it's only me, I'm ready for my G and T.
MAN: It's eight o'clock! You were gone so long, I worried there was something wrong.
(I thought you'd been run over by a bus or something.)
WOMAN: I beg your pardon, something wrong? Why on earth are you going on?
MAN: Well, my dear, look, all I mean, it's not your usual routine.
WOMAN: But, darling, take the time to remember
a conversation you recall,
when I informed you I would be later,
because I was going to the theatre.

(Vamp on F)

(It was really good, thanks for asking.)

MAN: *(looks genuinely puzzled)* That's not a thing I can recall.
I don't think it was me you spoke to.
You probably told your friend Maxine,
as she gets told life's details to the utmost degree!
WOMAN: I only phoned to let her know
I'd booked her a ticket for the show.
I can't believe we can talk at length,
and you have no recollection hence.
It goes to show what I've known all along:
you choose to be deaf when it suits you so.

CHORUS: He chooses to be deaf when it suits him so.

WOMAN: Why are men so annoyingly deaf?
When it comes to conversation I'm just wasting my breath.
They accuse you of prattling on and chatting at length,
then they'll hear the things they want to hear and disregard the rest.
MAN: (Pardon?)

WOMAN: Why are men so incredibly slow

To pick up on our signals that we blatantly show?
There are times I need a hug and some emotional drama,
but the best he'll do is make the tea then collapse to watch *Panorama*!
Why oh why can't you be more like me?
We'd really get along famously.

(Vamp on Dm)

MAN: (Aren't we over-reacting slightly?)
WOMAN: Ohhhh!
MAN: Now listen very carefully, here's something you'll agree on
That when God created man he had it all within his plan
to create a speciality, full of charming femininity.

(Vamp on F)

(Good we can laugh about our differences, isn't it?)

WOMAN: (Yes, darling, I suppose so – do you want to hear about the show I went to see? It was really rather good.)
MAN: (Yes, OK – that's reminds me of the time we went to London to see *The Mousetrap*, do you remember? In our wisdom we decided to drive in and you had control of the A-to-Z.)
WOMAN: *(through gritted teeth)* (Go on.)
MAN: I recall we set off early to avoid the hurly burly.
WOMAN: You faffed around till well past noon to avoid getting there a moment too soon!
MAN: Well, you had planned a mega shop to spend, spend, spend until I dropped.
WOMAN: That's a funny joke my dear, the creak of your wallet's not been heard for years.
MAN: But, darling, take the time to remember why I was such a dreadful bore. 'Cos you went into twenty-five dress shops, that made us late then bought the very first one you saw.
WOMAN: I recollect that dreadful date, I really wasn't all that choosy.
The only reason we missed the show
Was (be)cause you got us lost then wouldn't ask which way to go!

MAN: (I got us lost! I like that!)
I couldn't stop and ask directions on a red route with constant warden inspec-
tions.
I can't believe that you had the map laid out like a blanket across your lap!
It goes to show what I've known all along,
you are very dense when it suits you so.

CHORUS: She is very dense when it suits her so.

MAN: Why are women so incredibly dim?
When it comes to being logical they are off on a whim.
They will turn a map upside down to try and read directions,
then they'll send you wrong, still blaming you, with constant interjections.
Why do women show amazing passion?
You're suddenly more attractive once you're dressed in the latest fashion.
She will force you into tight new shoes when my slip-ons have barely crumbled,
whilst my nylon slacks and winceyettes have been bundled up for jumble!
(I've always found them very comfortable.)
Why oh why can't you be more like me?
We'd really get along famously.

(Vamp on F)

(He grins hopefully at her, she is not amused – ad lib if appropriate)

MAN: Just as well we're not the same …
WOMAN: life would be really rather tame.
MAN: If by chance I'm feeling blue …
WOMAN: … I know I can always count on you.
MAN: This I'll state quite honestly …
WOMAN: … you're still my cup of tea.
MAN: (Two sugars, thanks.)
WOMAN: Cup of tea! *(holding note)*
MAN: (And a gingernut wouldn't go amiss.)
WOMAN: Cup of tea! *(holding note, she sings higher and louder – cadenza, etc.)*
BOTH: And after all is said and done
You're still my number one!

New Beginnings

Words and music by Mandy Watsham

This ballad was written on New Year's Day 2000, with all the feelings from the night before still fresh in mind, and the sense of expectation that seemed to sweep the world regardless of whether or not people believed it to really be the dawn of a new millennium. There was something special about reaching the year 2000 – a milestone, perhaps – feeling united with those around us, inviting fresh starts and resolutions, being with people we cared about.

The essence of the song really reflects the freshness that people generally felt around that time – a sense of new beginnings – but the theme could also refer to several things – falling in love with someone special, weddings, new relationships or a new faith.

The song builds and changes key on the last chorus. Keep it simple at the start with a fairly light accompaniment, the drums providing a light rhythm and then gradually increasing in volume as the song builds.

The piece ends with preferably two or three voices in harmony singing 'in love tonight' a few times, until the soloist sings the final line: 'in love tonight now we're becoming one'.

New Beginnings

warmly ♩ = 66

D Solo instrument
Dmaj7
D6
Dmaj7

D
Dmaj7
D6
G   A7
p

1. There's a

D2
D/F♯
Asus4

spe - cial kind of ma - gic___ in the air up-on___ this night,   there's a
(2.) hope that springs e - ter - nal . . .

D
G
Asus4
A

feel - ing that the streets are paved with gold._____ There's a

D2
D/C♯
D/B
D/A

spe-cial kind of some - thing   in the   joy that fills_ our hearts,   like the

D
G
Asus4
A

sen - ti - ments of Christ - mas long_ a - go._____ You can

see it in the night sky, you can smell it on the breeze, oh, the sense

_ of ex - pec - ta - tion's_ soar - ing high._____ And I

know that you_ can feel_ it,_____ it's writ-ten on_ your face,

_____ the dawn-ing of_ a new age of his grace._____ And there's

no - where else on earth I'd real - ly ra - ther be_____ than to

spend it in_ your prec - ious com - pa - ny._____ There's a

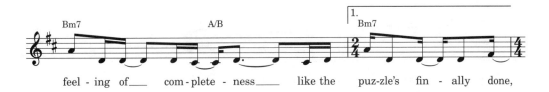

feel - ing of_ com - plete - ness_ like the puz - zle's fin - ally done,

Verse 1
There's a special kind of magic in the air upon this night,
there's a feeling that the streets are paved with gold.
There's a special kind of something in the joy that fills our hearts,
Like the sentiments of Christmas long ago.
You can see it in the night sky, you can smell it on the breeze,
Oh, the sense of expectation's soaring high.
And I know that you can feel it, it's written on your face,
The dawning of a new age of his grace.

Chorus
And there's nowhere else on earth I'd really rather be
than to spend it in your precious company
There's a feeling of completeness like the puzzle's finally done,
In love tonight now we're becoming one.

Verse 2
There's a hope that springs eternal from beyond the mists of time,
bubbling high above the embers of the past.
There's a light that's sparkling silver reflecting from the stars,
for the future and the love that can be ours.
There's a healthy optimism being echoed in the trees,
whilst the hope for peace is whispered on the breeze.
And I know that you can feel it, it's written on your face,
the dawning of a new age of his grace.

Chorus

(Instrumental, in new key of F)

Chorus

In love tonight, in love tonight, in love tonight, in love tonight,
in love tonight, in love tonight now we're becoming one.

Do I Look Fat in This?

Nicki Matthews

There have recently been a number of books written about the differences between men and women. This sketch takes a lighthearted look at how sometimes men and women seemingly speak totally different languages.

The action takes place in the living room of Melanie and Dave, a young married couple. Melanie arrives home from a shopping spree to find Dave engrossed in *Football Focus* or a similar football programme. Attempting to break into the action, Melanie asks Dave's opinion on her new outfits.

The sketch highlights some of the basic issues facing couples today. Dave appears not to listen to anything Melanie says, and Melanie clearly doesn't want Dave's real opinion, just confirmation of her own.

The football theme is continued through the sketch as an unseen commentator takes us through the action of the discussion and outlines how communication could have been improved, as per *Match of the Day* comments on goals and players.

It illustrates clearly how easy it is for communication to break down in relationships and the importance for couples to see things from the other's perspective. Although the sketch does not touch on the biblical teaching for relationships, it is an excellent springboard for a speaker to teach on the subject.

☺	☺	⏱
1	2	4 minutes

Other themes

Image, sport

Characters

MELANIE:	Young married woman
DAVE:	Her husband, football mad
VOICE:	Preferably male; in the style of a football commentator

Costumes

MELANIE:	Party dress with coat over the top
DAVE:	T-shirt and jeans

All you need

- ❑ Sofa (or two chairs with a throw over to look like one)
- ❑ Full shopping bags
- ❑ Two hats
- ❑ Optional sound effects: Saturday afternoon football from the TV, music (horror, à la *Psycho*)

(It is Saturday afternoon and DAVE is on the sofa watching the football. MELANIE appears, having returned from shopping laden with shopping bags.)

[football sound effect]

DAVE: Come on, you moron! I live nearer the goal than that pathetic excuse for a shot! What's the matter with you?

[sound of front door shutting]

MELANIE: *(from off-stage)* Hi, Dave! Can you come and help me with these bags? Dave? *(she trips through the door, dropping the bags. DAVE doesn't hear anything until she flops in the chair next to him)*

DAVE: *(without taking his eyes off the screen)* Oh hi, Mel, I didn't hear you come in. How was shopping?

MELANIE: A nightmare! You wouldn't believe the traffic queuing to get into the car park – it took me 45 minutes to find a space. *(as she speaks she is rummaging through her shopping bags)*

DAVE: NO WAY! *(facing TV screen)*

MELANIE: *(slightly amazed that he feels so strongly about her ordeal)* I know, but it was worth it. I'm sure this year's sales are better than usual – loads of bargains. I got these really nice gold boots …

DAVE: More boots! For goodness sake, Melanie, you have an obsession with footwear.

MELANIE: Not really …

DAVE: Melanie, the only people who can compete with you on the shoes and boots front are Clark's and Queen Imelda herself!

MELANIE: Anyway, shall I show you?

DAVE: Show me what?

MELANIE: What I bought!

DAVE: *(back watching the TV and reacting to a goal)* YES!

MELANIE: OK. *(goes off stage and talks as she's changing)* I couldn't make up my mind about the hat for Ben and Lyn's wedding, so I bought two. I can take one back. *(she appears with one hat on, holding the other)* So *(swapping hats to let him see)* which one do you like best?

[music sound effect, lights flash]

VOICE: *(as though coming from the football commentator)* Well, he has a choice here. Go for the blue to match the suit, or take a risk and try the cream. This is an important shot for Dave, it could change the direction of the future game.

DAVE: *(turning to her)* Ahh, umm, whichever you like, sweetheart.

MELANIE: Come on, Dave. *(swapping hats again)* Which is better? To go with my blue suit. The cream or blue?

DAVE: Um … *(crossing his fingers and hoping for the best)* … blue?

MELANIE: What's wrong with the cream, then?

DAVE: Cream, then – I don't mind.

MELANIE: You don't care, more like! I knew you wouldn't like the blue one – just 'cos it's twice the price! *(stomps out, slamming the door; off-stage, takes off coat to reveal new dress)*

DAVE: *(shouting after her)* If you don't want my opinion Melanie, don't ask for it! *(to himself)* For goodness sake – she can't make a decision herself, so I help her out and she moans. That's gratitude for you. I won't bother next time.

[MELANIE flounces in, wearing a new dress.]

MELANIE: I don't really know why I'm bothering, but what do you think of this dress? I got it for Emma's party next week. I don't look fat in it, do I?

[DAVE looks for a moment, to decide.]

[horror music sound effect, flashing lights again]

VOICE:	And Dave's just made another crucial mistake. He looked before answering!
MELANIE:	Oh, great, I obviously do.
DAVE:	I didn't say that – I was just looking …
MELANIE:	You'd know immediately if I looked slim, and as you had to think about I obviously look like an elephant! *(starting to get hysterical)* You always criticise what I'm wearing – if you ever notice, that is. I don't know why I bother asking, I really don't!
DAVE:	I'm saying nothing, 'cos whatever I say will be wrong!
VOICE:	Well, what a disappointing game there. Dave doesn't look like he's learnt anything at all since his signing five years ago – still making the same mistakes. And Melanie's still asking questions she doesn't want answers to. Let's have a look at an action replay of the highlights from the first half, with the benefits of hindsight and some extra training.

[DAVE resumes place in front of TV and MELANIE goes off stage, puts coat back on and appears in hats again.]

MELANIE:	*(swapping hats)* So Dave, which do you prefer, cream or blue?
VOICE:	It's important here not to give an answer.
DAVE:	Have you chosen the one you like, darling?
VOICE:	Good deflection. Opposition clearly taken aback by that, I think.
MELANIE:	Well, I think I like the cream …
VOICE:	Looks like she's gone for the cream.
DAVE:	Why cream?
MELANIE:	Well, I've got those new cream suede shoes which match it perfectly and that handbag your mum gave me for Christmas.
VOICE:	And the skilled response …
DAVE:	Wow, great choice. I agree. You'll look absolutely fabulous!
VOICE:	Great save. The whole tempo of the game has completely changed, and it looks like Dave's in with a great chance of scoring!

[Blackout]

Goodbye Mr Magnolia

Caroline Watsham

One woman's account of the breakdown of her marriage and how she is adjusting to her new circumstances.

After many years of a seemingly happy marriage, her middle-aged husband has recently left her for a younger member of the local amateur operatic society. The disloyalty of both her husband and so-called friend have left her, not surprisingly, somewhat bitter.

This is a poignant but humorous message of survival. It reminds us of the hurt and anguish sexual sin causes and the reasons why God's Word forbids it. It also, however, offers hope to those who find themselves in similar predicaments.

👤	👤	🕐
1	0	5 minutes

Other themes

Infidelity, starting afresh

Characters

BETTY: Middle-class, 40 to 50, articulate, genteel, perhaps a little
                staid

Costumes

Comfortable slacks and sweater, sensible shoes

All you need

❏ Chair
❏ Paint tin (needn't be full, but should look as though it contains shocking
   pink paint – perhaps from dribbles down the side)
❏ Paintbrush
❏ Radio sound effect – *The Archers* theme tune, or similar
❏ Radio/cassette player (optional)

[Closing bars of *The Archers* theme tune – Betty switches off radio]

BETTY: Do you know, I'm starting to appreciate how nice it is to listen to a whole episode without somebody taking it upon himself to punctuate each dramatic pause with a loud belch! Geoffrey never did like *The Archers*, but somehow he couldn't quite articulate his feelings in words.

He's been gone a month now – exactly a month.

It was so – so sudden. I really can't say there were any warning signs. I can't even remember any arguments over the years, unless you count the time we were redecorating and I ventured to suggest we opt for something slightly more adventurous than magnolia. There was a tense moment in the middle of B&Q before, as if bestowing an enormous favour, he picked up a couple of tins of 'rose white'. That's magnolia in my book, but I knew better than to pursue the matter.

Then one day last month, out of the blue, he announced he was leaving – came out with all this stuff about needing to 'find himself'. I said, 'What does that mean when it's at home?' He was floundering for words – the concept he was searching for obviously couldn't just be expressed by a bodily expulsion. 'Well, I've, er, just reached a point in my life where I'm not sure of who I am – it's just a matter of – er – finding myself.' Turns out he didn't have to look very hard – 'himself' was to be found five minutes down the road at Sandra's place!

Sandra Slatt. I know it doesn't do to speak ill of people, but if ever there was a woman with a typographical error for a surname, she's it. I remember the day she joined our amateur dramatic society – she walked into the hall and there was this sort of … frisson. A sort of eyes-out-on-stalks from the men and a bristling from the women. And that was before she'd so much as opened her mouth. Perhaps it was the high-heeled patent-leather boots she was wearing, despite having to make her way down a muddy track to the hall. Or maybe the blouse unbuttoned just one button below casual acquaintance level. Still, don't judge a book by its cover, I said to myself, and I resolved to welcome her to the group.

It wasn't actually a proper rehearsal night – we were holding auditions for our spring production, *Oklahoma*. I never bother auditioning myself, I usually end up as back row of the chorus anyway. Now to this day I don't know quite how it happened, but Sandra arrived a complete unknown and left at the end of the evening as Ado Annie, the 'girl who can't say no'. Geoffrey had the part of her boyfriend Will Parker – mind you that was pretty much a foregone conclusion as his only competition was Grandad Ron, who's pushing eighty and not in full control of his … you know … waterworks. Like most amateur groups, we have a serious shortage of men and a surplus of women, so I and the other ladies of a certain age were asked to make up the shortfall and be farmers or cowhands.

Not that Sandra's much younger than the rest of us – she just has a certain way about her that defies even the hardest director to cast her as anything but female.

I tried to see the funny side – I remember remarking to Geoffrey that 'the girl who can't say no' was quite apt, seeing we'd learned that Sandra had just completed her third divorce. I didn't quite catch what he said – something like 'better than a girl who can't say yes', or something.

It was shortly after Christmas that he started going to extra rehearsals at Sandra's place. I was busy with my WI. Don't get me wrong, we're not the new breed who bare their all on calendars! No, it's all respectable stuff, I assure you. I was quite impressed with the effort he was putting in, and it gave me a bit of space to get on with my marmalade-making. I did think it was a bit odd, though, when he grew a moustache and then went and bought some tight jeans – I mean, I'd only just given him a pair of beige slacks for Christmas.

I had to laugh when I came into the bedroom and found him flat on the floor with a coathanger through the zip, heaving and straining, trying to get them done up. When he finally managed, he had to sort of ease himself up to the vertical, then it took him ten minutes to creak down the stairs! *(She laughs, but the laugh catches in her throat and she blinks back a tear.)*

I suppose what really hurts is the betrayal of our friendship – I mean, we'd been together long enough for all that passion stuff to have gone off a bit – but I thought we'd settled into something comfortable, like a favourite pair of slippers.

Come showtime, Sandra delighted in flouncing about in her low-cut costume in front of us lady cowboys – we even had to stick on beards and moustaches, it took weeks for the glue to completely wash off. Anyway, dress rehearsal I come out of the dressing room in my full John Wayne regalia, see Geoffrey leaning in what he fondly imagines is a nonchalant pose against the wall, so I do a little twirl, just for a laugh. Sandra appears and stage-whispers to him something about poking and cows, and he falls about laughing. It's not that I can't take a joke, but there was something about the quality of the laughter – it was *at* me rather than *with* me. And his eyes – he was looking at me as if I was a stranger, not the woman he'd been married to for twenty years. Suddenly, I'd become an embarrassing inconvenience to him, and he obviously chose to forget I had a brain or feelings. It sounds like such a trivial incident, but the hurt still sticks in my mind – much more than the feelings I had when he finally told me he was leaving.

Sorry to get maudlin. I'm still in shock in a way. But, you know, a friend of mine said something the other day that really got me thinking. She said, 'Betty, God never gives you more than you can cope with.' I thought, 'Well, I'm flattered, your Almightiness, by your high opinion of my resilience, and I suppose in the biblical scale of catastrophes this ranks rather lower than a flood, or a plague of locusts, but still …' But do you know, I want to think I can cope. I don't know how yet, but I'll just take one day at a time. In fact, I've made a promise to myself – every day I write in my diary one good thing to have come of all this. Granted, they're quite small things at the moment. The first entry, which occurred to me within a couple of days of his departure, was 'Had the duvet to myself all night – no 3.00 a.m.

tug of war!' Then there was the realisation that I don't have to spend half of Sunday toiling over a roast lunch and the other half tidying the kitchen. Oh, and that reminds me – today's entry *(she writes)* 'Goodbye Mr Magnolia!'

Come on, Betty, on your feet. It's time for a bit of colour about the place. *(From behind the chair she lifts the paint pot and brandishes the brush.)*

Listen with Mother

Mandy Watsham and Nicki Matthews

This sketch is a conversation between an elderly mother and her middle-aged daughter, who has come to visit. Despite rarely seeing each other, neither of them seems to be particularly interested in the other's life.

Jean has come to tell her mother that she is getting a divorce from her husband Jim because of his philandering. Unfortunately her mother is slightly deaf, and most of the conversation passes with her totally misunderstanding the point. Jean is clearly upset by her husband's actions and is looking for some support from her mother. But her mother's deafness, coupled with her absorption in her own problems, does not allow her to give Jean that support, and they part as if they have not even met.

A sad indication of how family relationships can deteriorate if we don't give them the time they deserve.

👩	🧍	🕐
2	0	5 minutes

Other themes

Old age, divorce, infidelity, world of TV

Characters

JEAN: Rather 'tired with life' middle-aged wife and mother whose husband has left her – too wrapped up in her own problems to worry about her mother.

MOTHER: Sad and lonely pensioner who rarely gets visits from her family and as such is no longer interested in them. The soaps on TV seem more real to her than her own family's problems.

Costumes

JEAN: Middle-class, middle-aged outfit, such as coat and boots if winter, sun dress and strappy sandals if summer

MOTHER: Blouse, cardigan and skirt with thick 'American tan' tights and slippers. Rug over knees, glasses.

All you need

❏ Armchair (or simple chair with a throw over to look like one)
❏ Remote control
❏ Sound effects: theme music for *Coronation Street*

[Scene opens with MOTHER watching television]

JEAN: *(from off-stage)* Hello, Mummy, it's only me.

[MOTHER has obviously not heard anything and ignores JEAN.]

JEAN: *(appearing)* Hello, Mummy, it's only me. *(Kisses her on the cheek and sits down)*

MOTHER: Oh hello, Jean dear, I didn't hear you come in. Just hang on a bit would you – I think I know the answer to this one. *(Shouting at the TV)* It's Helsinki, you stupid man! *(muttering)* Ridiculous! He's just lost £250.

             Fancy not knowing that! *(turns TV off with remote)*

JEAN: So, Mum, how have you been?

[MOTHER has obviously not heard and sits smiling expectantly, waiting for her to speak.]

JEAN: *(speaking very loudly and slowly)* SO, MUM, HOW ARE YOU?

MOTHER: Oh, you know. *(pathetically)* Same as usual. *(slightly wheezing)* My chest still isn't right. I've had the doctor out but he just tells me I'm an old woman – as if I didn't know! And my legs! Well, some days it feels as if someone is using a huge screwdriver to tighten the joints in my knees – can you imagine what that's like, Jean? A screwdriver at your kneecaps all night? No, you probably can't – you're still young. But, of course, my knees are nothing compared to my problems *(mouthing and pointing)* down below. You wouldn't believe …

JEAN: *(interrupting)* Mummy, I need to talk to you!

MOTHER: Pardon? *(fiddling with hearing aid)*

JEAN: *(louder)* I said I need to talk to you.

MOTHER: Well, go on, then – get on with it.

JEAN: *(shamefacedly)* Well, it's a bit difficult … it's just … well, basically, Jim and I, we're getting a divorce.

[MOTHER, smiling, has obviously not heard anything. JEAN looks slightly puzzled by the lack of reaction.]

MOTHER: I can't hear a word you're saying, dear, but I'm sure it's fascinating.

JEAN: I said *(louder)* Jim and I are getting a divorce.

MOTHER: *(looks puzzled; then, incredulously)* What on earth for?

JEAN: *(slightly surprised at the strength of reaction from her mother)* Well, we haven't been getting on very well recently.

MOTHER: Well, how on earth is this going to help?

JEAN: Well, we thought a bit of space would do us good.

MOTHER: I should think you will need a bit of space – a great deal of space indeed. How on earth are you going to get that living in the middle of London?

JEAN: Well, Jim has moved out.

MOTHER: Yes, I agree, he always was a bit of a lout, but what does that have to do with getting extra space?

JEAN: No, I said he's *(louder)* MOVED OUT.

MOTHER: Well, that's not going to be enough, is it? You'll need at least an acre.

JEAN: *(looks puzzled but decides not to ask and ignores the comment)* The thing is, Mummy *(getting a bit upset)* Jim's had an affair.

MOTHER: Yes, they do have a lot of hair, don't they. I used to have a sofa stuffed with it once. They were all the rage when your father and I first married. Jolly uncomfortable though – did terrible things to my haemorrhoids, I remember …

[During this little speech JEAN has been looking more and more puzzled and eventually interrupts.]

JEAN: What on earth are you talking about?

MOTHER: Well, I know I was young to have them but …

JEAN: No, I mean why are you talking about horse-hair sofas?

MOTHER:	Well, it was you talking about your new horse – got me thinking about it.
JEAN:	What new horse? *(now quite incredulous)*
MOTHER:	Yours and Jim's new horse.
JEAN:	We haven't got a new horse. *(almost at screaming pitch)*
MOTHER:	You said you and Jim were getting a horse. *(adamant)*
JEAN:	*(realisation suddenly hits)* NOT A HORSE! A DIVORCE! *(then to herself)* You deaf old bat. *(shouting)* A DIVORCE, A DIVORCE. JIM'S MOVING OUT TO LIVE WITH HIS FANCY WOMAN. A DIVORCE, NOT HORSE. WHY ON EARTH WOULD I GET A HORSE? I LIVE IN ISLINGTON, FOR GOODNESS SAKE!
MOTHER:	Well, that's what I thought, and there's no need to shout – I'm not deaf!

[JEAN shakes her head in disbelief.]

MOTHER:	Well, I am glad you're not getting a horse, and quite frankly I'm not at all surprised to see that Jim go. I never warmed to him – eyes too close together for my liking …
JEAN:	*(interrupting and rather weary now)* Anyway, I just wanted to let you know. Thanks for the chat, I really needed to talk things over with you. I feel much better now.*(getting up)*
MOTHER:	*(hasn't heard the last comments)* Oh, are you off? Well, thanks for coming, love. Sorry I couldn't offer you a cup of tea or anything, *(wearily)* but it's such an effort to get up these days. Like I said, there's not much I can do – I just have to grin and bear it.
JEAN:	Well, I'll pop in and see you again when I can. Hope you feel better tomorrow. *(Kisses her on the cheek and exits)*
MOTHER:	Thank goodness for that, I thought she'd never go – wittering on about horses all night! *(switches on TV and we hear* Coronation Street *theme music)* Great! Now I'll *never* know how Ken and Deirdre got back together!

[Blackout]

Mid-Morning with Ken and Jen

Mandy Watsham and Nicki Matthews

This sketch is a skit on day-time magazine television programmes.

It encompasses a phone-in on relationships and serves to highlight a very obvious problem in Ken and Jen's relationship, based on a lack of communication. (You could change the phone-in to suit your chosen subject if wished.)

NB: Because of the natural gaps in this script, you can use the show as the vehicle for a whole presentation and insert music, videos and testimonies, as appropriate.

🧍‍♀️	🧍	🕐
5*	1	6 minutes

*(3 if Muriel/Susie and Annie/Rachel double up)

Other themes

TV

Characters

KEN:	Rather 'full of himself' TV presenter, about 35, arrogant
JEN:	His wife. Much more in touch with her audience. Similar age
MURIEL:	Resident agony aunt
SUSIE:	Resident cook
YVONNE:	First caller in phone-in. About to have a baby.
ANNIE:	Second caller in phone-in, with problem daughter.
RACHEL:	Third caller in phone-in, problems with boyfriend.

Costumes

KEN:	Chinos and open-necked shirt
JEN:	Trouser suit
MURIEL:	Something granny-like and homely.
SUSIE:	Anything with an apron or chef's whites over the top.

All you need

❏ Two chairs
❏ Yellow notes/scripts

KEN: Good morning and welcome to the show. And before we go any
         further I want to state that I've decided that today is casual day.
         I'm going tie-less. I've said, 'Blow it, I've worn a shirt and tie for
         ten years and it's time for a change.' So before you ring and ask
         why isn't Ken wearing a tie, and I know you will, let's get that
         straight. OK.

JEN: *(looking fed up)* Right, coming up in today's show …

KEN: *(interrupts)* … an interesting look at today's trend for DIY
         programmes. Do we get enough of them? *(looks serious)*

JEN: And our resident cook Susie will be cooking up a Mediterranean
         treat with scrumptious tahini.

KEN: I don't like fish!

JEN: It's not a fish, darling, it's a nut paste!

KEN: I knew that. And following on from that, our phone-in. An
         interesting one today, on love, relationships and families. So if
         you have any problems of a *personal* nature … call us now on
         395794758947. Is the number up? Oh, let's wait. *(obviously
         irritated with the technical crew)* Is it up? *(tapping fingers)* Live
         TV, folks. It's there, now is it? THANK YOU.

JEN: But let's first of all go over to a song with our musical guests this
         morning …

KEN: Yes, I discovered them …

[break for song or video, if appropriate]

KEN: Right, let's go to the phone-in. Line 1, you've got an interesting
         problem, haven't you? Sorry, what's your name? Yvonne. Right.
         You've had a baby …

YVONNE: Well, no I haven't, actually, I'm due in six days.

KEN: Oh sorry, I've been given the wrong facts … AGAIN. Carry on!

YVONNE: Well, it's actually quite a serious problem …

KEN: Actually, just before we get to that *(smiling excitedly)* can I just
         ask you what you think about MY idea of the team putting

together their own band for a performance live on the show, 'cos I don't know if you're aware but I'm quite a vocalist and a pretty mean guitar player.

YVONNE: Well, you have quite a lot of musical guests so ... I'm not sure if it is a good idea.

KEN: Really? Well, you're the only one out of – how many calls have we had today – yes ... well ... a lot. So ... I believe we have a call now on line 2. Hello line 2, how can we help?

JEN: Oh, we seem to have lost Yvonne. Stay on the line, love, and we'll get Muriel (gesturing to MURIEL), our agony aunt and trained counsellor, to speak to you later. Right now it's Annie on line 2. How can we help, love?

ANNIE: Well, I'm worried about my daughter. Her behaviour has become quite erratic.

JEN: In what way, love? Take your time if it's easier.

KEN: We're behind schedule.

JEN: *(glaring at KEN)* Go ahead, pet.

ANNIE: Well, every Thursday she'd come in from school and do her homework and then sit down and watch *Neighbours*.

JEN: Mmm. *(looking very caring)*

KEN: What is it – not doing her homework any more?

ANNIE: No, it gets worse – she'll come in, do her homework and then start watching *Hollyoaks*, closely followed by *Brookside*.

KEN: Continue.

ANNIE: Well, I'm sure you two will understand – I mean, you moved away from there to live down south, presumably for the same reason that I'm worried about.

KEN: *(tiring now as he struggles to keep interested in the plot)* Which is?

ANNIE: Well, isn't it obvious? I mean, I'm petrified that she'll pick up a Scouse accent!

KEN: Yes, I realised that!

JEN: Oh, you poor love. Muriel?

MURIEL: Well …

KEN: *(interrupts* MURIEL *and gives his own opinion – obviously has no idea at all)* Can I just say I think the best thing is to make sure you send her to a GOOD school, provide her with lots of good reading matter – Shakespeare, Hardy, Tolkien … er … *(running out of names)* Enid Blyton … Promote a healthy interest in needlework, tapestry, cross-stitch, and so on, take her swimming twice a week in a private pool, and occasionally take her pot-holing or rock-climbing with the Somerset WI. I think that's the next best answer to chucking the TV out or leaving the country, frankly.

JEN: Thanks for that darling. Annie, has that in any way helped, love? *(mouthing to* MURIEL, *'I can't believe it could have done')* Annie, love?

ANNIE: *(crying with despair and then saying almost madly with abandonment)* Yes. Yes, that's helped so much, yes, thank you, Ken …Yes, yes, yes … *(gets cut off in mid-hysterics)*

KEN: *(not realising he's driven the poor woman mad, looking smug)* Great. Do you know, it's frightening when you're always right!

JEN: *(cutting in quickly)* Line 3 now.

RACHEL: Well, I've been going out with my new boyfriend for three weeks and we went swimming the other day.

KEN: Go on, love. *(nodding in a concerned fashion as though he knows what's coming next)*

RACHEL: It was the first time I'd seen him naked and his body is just covered in moles. I just find it very unattractive. We get on really well but his moles make me feel physically ill. I just don't know what to do about it. Am I fickle?

KEN: Um, that's a problem. What do you think, Muriel?

MURIEL: I really don't know how to help you, love.

JEN: Well, I don't know what the problem is. *(to* KEN*)* You're quite moley, aren't you!

KEN: I am not!

JEN: Yes you are, there's that big one on your back – I quite like it.

KEN: Well, good for you, glad you like them, but I'm not moley, I haven't got any moles – not that there's anything particularly wrong with having moles if you happen to be unlike me and happen to have any. Don't phone in complaining about that one.

JEN: You have! So, caller …

KEN: I'm not moley.

JEN: Well, we could suggest plasters …

MURIEL: Or a good solid foundation – I use a great one. You'd never guess I was 92.

JEN: And we love you, pet – you're brilliant, just like a mum to me. *(JEN starts to well up)*

KEN: *(cutting in hurriedly)* Other than that – no idea.

JEN: *(annoyed he's cut an emotional moment)* Let's ask the moliest man I know. Ken, what do you do?

KEN: Nothing, I do nothing 'cos I haven't got any moles. Right, we're out of time on that, I'm afraid. Let's take a break …

[music starts]

KEN: *(speaking over music)* Fancy saying I'm moley. I'm not at all moley. *(etc., etc.)*

[music]

KEN: Welcome back. Now before we go on, I have a very serious issue to deal with. Last night, Jen and I were having dinner in our local restaurant – thanks, Marcel, for a great meal, you're a real pal. Unfortunately it was spoiled by some petty, small-minded, ignorant, jealous *(running out of insults and knowing he can't swear on TV)* banana head, who took it upon themselves to ring the police and report me for drink driving. Now I never drink and drive. Do I, Jen?

JEN: Well …

KEN: I don't. And when I leave the restaurant there's a police car lying in wait 200 yards down the road. They breathalysed me, but of course they didn't find a trace of alcohol. But whoever you are – and I've a good idea who you are, no, I KNOW who you are – I won't be letting this drop. I'm on your case. *(silence)* Let's go to a break.

JEN: We've just had a break.

KEN: Right, then it must be Susie and the cookery slot? *(SUSIE is seen offstage with a cup of tea chatting to the floor manager)* No, right, didn't think so. OK, I think we've got a VT to show. Sorry, technical term for video. About spider plants – the new fashion accessory.

[video; incorrect video is played or no video is played – there is obviously a technical hitch]

KEN: Right. Don't phone in – we know that was the wrong tape. And let me reassure you that the person responsible – Tony Griffiths – knows he is in deep trouble and as we speak is collecting his P45. Muriel, love, you might need to be on hand for a bit of counselling later on.

MURIEL: *(just about to say OK)*

KEN: On second thoughts, don't worry. I'll do it. I'm probably more experienced in these matters. OK, right, coming up later a fantastic band – our very own mid-morning team with me on lead vocals and lead guitar, Muriel on tambourine and … sorry, love, what are you doing again?

JEN: *(managing a tight smile)* But first we are now ready for our cookery slot and more of the Best of British. Right, Susie, I've really been looking forward to this. It sounds delicious. What is it?

KEN: *(makes his way over to the table)*

SUSIE: Well, it's …

KEN: Sorry, I'm going to have to hurry you …

SUSIE: Oh, OK. Well, here's one I started earlier …

KEN: No, really, running out of time …

SUSIE: *(throws everything together)*

KEN: Sorry, we've got 15 seconds left to tell the viewers the crucial ingredients.

SUSIE: Right, well …

KEN: I'm going to have to hurry you.

SUSIE: Twenty-five grams …

KEN: Come on!

SUSIE: … of butter …

KEN: Three, two, one, sorry, that's it. If you want the recipe – hard luck. We're out of time.

SUSIE: *(is busy throwing the remaining ingredients down and stomping off to the floor manager to moan about KEN – goes off gesticulating)*

KEN: But before the end of this show we've just got time for our team band slot. So, thanks for watching, see you next week, and take it away, team!

[Two endings: either KEN heads off to band and they play out, or he goes over, but just as he's about to start the theme music starts signalling the end of the show and he's cut off. Floor manager can start applause as theme music plays out. Blackout.]

Good to Talk

David Robinson

This sketch, the title of which is a play on the BT catchphrase, is simply an illustration of how we forget to communicate with the people we think we know best.

The sketch is set in a pub, represented by a small table stage left where Brian and Sue are having their regular drink together. They have been together for eleven years, and for those eleven years have spent every Saturday night at the same pub having the same drinks and crisps until 9.30 p.m., when they go home to watch *Match of the Day*.

This particular evening, Brian is remembering an incident two weeks previously, when out of the blue Sue commented that she would like to do something else for a change.

The ensuing conversation is a comical look at how we can take people for granted, and highlights the fact that communication is key in all relationships.

🧍‍♀️	🧍	🕐
1	1	5 minutes

Other themes

Family life

Characters

SUE:	Forty-something
BRIAN:	A year or so older than Sue

Costumes

SUE:	Neat and tidy but unimaginative casual clothes
BRIAN:	Jacket and baggy-kneed cords, V-necked pullover

All you need

❏ Small pub table
❏ (Optional) two trays of drinks: one holding lager, grapefruit juice and bag of plain crisps; one holding lager, apple juice and bag of beef and onion crisps. Business with drinks could be mimed for simplicity

[BRIAN is downstage right addressing the audience. SUE is seated, very sourfaced, at a small pub table, stage left.]

BRIAN: … I mean, we come in here every Saturday night – have done for the last eleven years – always have done. We're known in here. Brian and Sue, the Green Man, every Saturday night, eight till nine-thirty. We always have two rounds, a pint of lager and a grapefruit juice first time, and a pint of lager, a grapefruit and a packet of plain crisps second round. She can never finish a packet so she does what she can and I do the rest.

Two weeks ago I take the drinks back to the table. (BRIAN *takes the drinks back.*) We sit there for twenty minutes as usual, not saying a word to each other. And then I turned to Sue and I said, 'Well, come on, love, it's half past nine. Drink up, it's *Match of the Day* in twenty minutes.' She sat there in silence for a minute and then she says …

SUE: Just something different, that's all I ask for – something different.

BRIAN: Yer what?

SUE: Something different, Brian, that's all I ask for. Something a bit different in my life.

BRIAN: Why change something if you like what you're doing? You like being here, you like the Green Man, you like grapefruit juice, you like plain crisps, you always have done. So what do you want to change things for?

SUE: How do you know I don't want to change things? You've never asked me.

BRIAN: I don't need to ask, I can tell just looking at you that you're happy.

SUE: Pineapple juice. I'd just like pineapple juice one week instead of grapefruit. That's all.

BRIAN: Well, why didn't you tell me? I am quite capable of going up to the bar and asking for a pineapple juice. You just need to tell me and I will go up to the bar and then I could come back to this table with a pineapple juice and not grapefruit. And then you can have pineapple juice.

SUE:	I want you to surprise me.
BRIAN:	You don't like surprises.
SUE:	I do.
BRIAN:	You don't. Last month coming back from your sister's in Leicester, I come off the motorway, you're fast asleep in the back, I say, 'Come on, I'll treat you to dinner here – save you cooking when we get home.'
SUE:	I'd only just woken up. *(BRIAN goes back to the bar.)* I needed to do my make-up, my hair, put something smart on, get myself prepared.
BRIAN:	I mean, I ask you! Make-up, hair, smart clothes … Burger King at Newport Pagnell services. For goodness sake! I thought I'd get one up on her this week. *(goes back to the table)* There we are, love, apple juice and a packet of beef and onion. Don't say I never surprise you.
SUE:	Onions give me indigestion, Brian, and you know it. *(she goes out in disgust)* If you eat those don't come back breathing all over me.
BRIAN:	With that she was off. I didn't rush after her. I just sat there and finished off a pint of lager, a packet of beef and onion and an apple juice. Quite pleasant, actually. I sat there looking at my beer mat, trying the best I could to understand women. In the end I just gave myself a migraine. So I got home eventually, went into the kitchen, got myself a cup of tea and a biscuit, and then I went into the front room to join Sue. Now – and here is the real icing on the cake – she wasn't even watching *Match of the Day*. Said she'd never wanted to watch *Match of the Day* and was quite enjoying some soppy drama on ITV, thanks very much. I mean, I just couldn't believe it. All she had to do was say something. I mean, we've done everything together, always have done. We've even worked together for years. Yes, we both work for British Telecom, have done since we left college. We've always been involved in communications. Well, I mean, it's good to talk, isn't it?

(At bar) All right, Jim, that's a packet of pork scratchings, a bag of dry roasteds and a large pina colada, please.

[Lights fade]

CHAPTER 10

there must be a better way to continue the human race?

Parenthood, children and family life

This section includes three songs and four sketches based around the subject of family life, including being a mother, having babies and even the possibility of men giving birth!

If your presentation is based around Mother's Day or Father's Day, or if you are simply choosing the subject of parenthood, you will surely find something to suit your programme here.

SONGS

- ❏ A Mother's Love
- ❏ Our Lives Go On
- ❏ Let It Rain

SCRIPTS

Leave Maternity
A dinner party with four friends celebrating Jonathan's birthday. He and his wife Maria are career people and their friends have a growing family. As the sketch goes on, it becomes clear that Maria's career may not be enough and that perhaps children should be part of their future.

Who'd Be Mother?
A fly-on-the-wall observation of a scene in a 'normal' family home somewhere between teatime and bedtime. Busy mum Lisa is having a conversation on the phone with a friend but is constantly interrupted by her children of various ages.

Millennium Newsdesk – Headline: 'Pregnant Man'
News report from 2034 including the breaking story of the first man to give birth.

Hats
An illustration of how many roles the average wife and mother fulfils in a normal day.

A Mother's Love

Words and music by Mandy Watsham and Nicki Matthews

For Judith and Jeanne

This easy-listening piece starts by playing the chorus as its introduction. After eight bars, verse 1 begins.

The song is all about mothers and that natural, inexplicable bond they have with their children, the unselfish nature of being a mother – 'you gave love away, you never withheld, willing to give all you had'.

The chorus simply sings that even though we're now grown up and perhaps are parents ourselves, we still have a deep-rooted need for our mother's love, and sometimes we still 'need you now today, maybe more than yesterday'. Sometimes there are times in our lives when only our mum will do!

The bridge talks about how 'your love shaped this child for life, by what you gave away', and then brings in the parallels of the love of our Father God when it says 'as our Father God loves us so I can see a glimpse of him reflecting through the love in your eyes'.

Perhaps the song suggests that a mother or father's love is a gift from God, as he is the one who created love and families. And the love our mothers feel for us and we feel for our own children is a reflection of the enormous love that God feels for us, his own children.

A Mother's Love

♩ = 100

1. Then, back in the days____ when I was small,__ you__ were there.
2. You ne-ver with-held . . .
3. Where would I be now . . .

__ You helped me to walk,__ helped me to talk,_____ to

stand____ on my own feet, how to suc - ceed__ with-out your help,

__ with - out need,__ you gave love a - way.__

1. Oh__

2. But I__ CHORUS

Verse 1
Then, back in the days when I was small, you were there.
You helped me to walk, helped me to talk,
to stand on my own feet,
how to succeed without your help, without need,
You gave love away.

Verse 2
You never withheld, willing to give all you had.
You sacrificed self, to give me the things you perceived would help me grow,
encouraged my gifts, honed my desires, cheered me on,
You gave love away

Chorus
But I need you now today,
maybe more than yesterday,
I need you, 'cos there's things that only you can understand.
You're the one who gave me life,
you're the one who'll make things right,
you're the only one – I must concede,
there's times I need to feel a mother's love.

Verse 3
Where would I be now without the love that you shared?
You see my success, all I've achieved, as the proof that your job's done.
I'm on my own, discovered my wings and I've flown.
You gave me away

Chorus

Bridge
Your love shaped this child for life
by what you gave away.
As our Father God loves us
so I can see a glimpse of him
reflecting through the love in your eyes,
in your eyes.

Chorus

Oh how I need to feel my mother's love.

Our Lives Go On

Music by Mandy Watsham, words by Maddy Barnet

This song uses the words of a poem written by a family member who tragic-ally lost her father to cancer. She read this poem at the funeral, and the words were so beautiful and heartfelt that as I read them a tune seemed to fit them perfectly.

It's a very short piece and could be used as an interlude, or to follow a drama or film clip. The introduction is written in F and is designed to be played with a certain amount of freedom and smoothness of style. The first part of the vocals continues the smooth uninterrupted style of the introduction, but when it gets to 'so when we ask and we're not told' the volume increases and stronger tone is required, fading gradually from 'with this courage in our minds our lives go on' and singing the last note open and straight on a diminuendo.

The words talk about how 'in our hearts and minds he will live on', remem-bering his courage in the face of adversity and his unfailing sense of humour.

Our Lives Go On

Ballad – Ethereal ♩ = 62

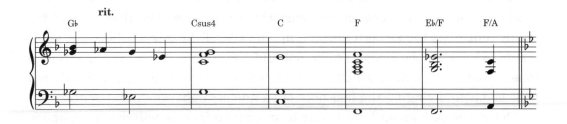

We can all ask why but won't be told, say good-bye and then we'll

still feel cold. But I know from what he said— is that it's on - ly in

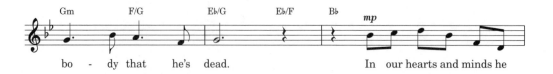

bo — dy that he's dead. In our hearts and minds he

will   live on,   and the mark he made for - ev - er will be strong.

He made us laugh, he made us   cry,   and this is   what   I   will re -

- mem - ber him   by.   So when we ask and we're not   told,____

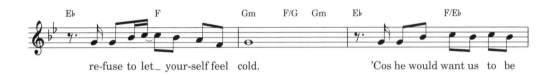

re-fuse to let_ your-self feel   cold.   'Cos he would want us to be

strong,   and with this cour - age   in our   minds   our_ lives____   go

on. ____

We can all ask why but won't be told,
say goodbye and then we'll still feel cold.
But I know from what he said
is that it's only in body that he's dead.

In our hearts and minds he will live on,
and the mark he made forever will be strong.
He made us laugh, he made us cry,
and this is what I will remember him by.

So when we ask and we're not told,
refuse to let yourself feel cold.
'Cos he would want us to be strong,
and with this courage in our minds
our lives go on.

Let It Rain

Words and music by Mandy Watsham and Nicki Matthews

This piece has been written in the style of Jewish song. The music and chords reflect those used in traditional Jewish music.

The chorus is written in 4/4, changing to 3/4 for the verses. The piece gradually builds to become stronger and louder, finishing if possible with Jewish type wailing/ad libbing at the end.

The theme is children, specifically children living in life-threatening situations. Verse 1 refers to the children of Guatemala and is inspired by the work of the Toybox charity. Verse 2 is based on the children from war-torn Bosnia and the information we receive from our friends at Novimost International, a charity working with them in the former Yugoslavia. Verse 3 is based on children in the African nations: at some point in our lives we have all seen and been touched by the images of starvation in Africa that appear regularly on our TV screens.

The song highlights their plight but also states that 'someone who knows what it's like to feel pain, to live in the shadow of death, cares and respects you so hold your head high'.

Jesus loves each of us equally, regardless of our nationality, wealth or social position, and he feels our pain intensely. Each one of these little children matters to him. The rain in the chorus could refer to the physical relief – providing aid, help, love – that we could bring these children, or to them knowing love of Jesus, which brings hope, eternal relief and peace.

Let It Rain

VERSES

1. Scra-ping a life from the scraps that they find, sol-diers with
2. Liv-ing in fear . . .
3. Will some-one bring . . .

guns who will fire._____ Fright-ened of day-light, the_ threat on their

lives, scared lone-ly child-ren who cry. Who real-ly

1.
cares?_____

2.
cares?_____

D.$.

3.
_ Let it cares?_____

BRIDGE

Some-one who knows what it's like to feel pain, to live in the

sha-dow of death,_____ loves and res - pects you so

hold your head high, trust in his un-fail-ing love, safe in his

care._____ Let it rain____ on the child-ren,___ let it

pour on their need. Let it flow for their in-no-cent hearts, send some

rain for their re-lease.__ On-ly then will they_ know peace._____

Let it

Aah_____ aah_____

_____ aah_____ aah_____

Chorus
Let it rain on the children,
let it pour on their need.
Let it flow for their innocent hearts,
send some rain for their release.
Only then can they find peace.

Verse 1
Scraping a life from the scraps that they find,
soldiers with guns who will fire.
Frightened of daylight, the threat on their lives,
scared lonely children who cry.
Who really cares?

Verse 2
Living in fear of the shells that might fall,
watching the door every night.
Fathers and brothers have already gone.
Children who've witnessed despair
ask, 'Who will care?'

Chorus

Verse 3
Will someone bring us the food that we need?
Surely there's plenty to spare?
Babies are dying – there's barely enough.
Children with nothing ask why
nobody cares.

Bridge
Someone who knows what it's like to feel pain,
to live in the shadow of death,
loves and respects you so hold your head high,
trust in his unfailing love,
safe in his care.

Chorus x 2

Leave Maternity

Nicki Matthews

This sketch is centred on a dinner party with four friends celebrating Jonathan's birthday. He and his wife Maria are career people who made a decision early on in their relationship that they did not want to have children. Their friends Elaine and Gordon, on the other hand, have a growing family.

As the sketch goes on, we witness a private conversation between Maria and Elaine in the kitchen, when Elaine announces that she is pregnant again. It then starts to become clear that all the material wealth she and Jonathan have amassed together may not be enough for Maria, and that perhaps children should be part of their future. A similar conversation between Jonathan and Gordon in the dining room, however, indicates that Jonathan is not of a similar mind to Maria.

Despite Maria's insistence that she does not want go back on her agreement with her husband, Elaine insists that she talks to Jonathan, illustrating the importance of communication in relationships.

👧	🧍	🕐
2	2	8 minutes

Other themes

Relationships, materialism

Characters

MARIA: Successful career woman of about 30. Partner in a firm of solicitors who has achieved all the targets she set herself. For the first time in her life she thinks she might want a baby

JONATHAN: Her husband, has successfully built up his own architect's firm. Enjoys golf and working out down at the gym. Confident character, both in his appearance and in what he has achieved. Doesn't want a family

ELAINE: Maria's best friend. She already has a child and wants nothing more than to build a family with husband Gordon

GORDON: Married to Elaine, he has similar family values. Works hard for a living, but has not been as successful as his friend Jonathan because of his family commitments

Costumes

MARIA: Smart black dress, simple but elegant
JONATHAN: Classy open-neck shirt and trousers
ELAINE: Trousers and top – nothing too fancy
GORDON: Conservative shirt and tie and trousers

All you need

❏ Table and four chairs
❏ Candle for centre of table
❏ Four wine glasses filled with wine
❏ Four bowls and spoons to indicate they have finished pudding
❏ Tea tray with four cups
❏ Table for kitchen with kettle, tea bags and coffee
❏ Bottle of port

[Lights up on all four characters seated at the dining room table]

GORDON: So, everyone – compliments to the chef!

ELAINE: Yes, that was a wonderful meal, Maria.

GORDON: And happy birthday, Jonathan!

[All three raise their glasses and wish happy birthday, etc.]

GORDON: So, how does it feel to be an old man?

JONATHAN: Do you mind! I'm only two years older than you and I bet I could outrun you on the badminton court any day!

GORDON: Yes, you probably could. Actually I'm fairly unfit these days. I never seem to get the time for exercise.

MARIA: Well, I wasn't going to mention your belly, Gordon, but as you've brought it up! *(laughs)*

GORDON: *(pulls in his stomach; sarcastically)* Thank you for that my dear! Weren't you going to make coffee?

MARIA: Yes I was, wasn't I. Everyone want coffee or does anyone prefer tea?

ELAINE: Actually, have you got any fruit teas? It's just that I've gone right off tea and coffee at the moment.

MARIA: I think I've got a box of camomile somewhere in the back of the cupboard. It's left from when Jonathan started this health kick!

JONATHAN: Oh yes, I remember. Foul, they were! I'm all for healthy eating but I draw the line at those.

ELAINE: Camomile's fine, thanks, Maria. I'll come and help you, shall I?

[They collect up the bowls from the table and move stage left to 'kitchen'.]

MARIA: *(making drinks)* So what's the deal with coffee and tea? Usually you drink buckets of it.

ELAINE: Well, we weren't going to mention it tonight. After all it is Jon's birthday and we didn't want to steal the limelight. But ... what the heck! I'm pregnant again!

MARIA:	Oh Elaine, that's wonderful news. Billy will be so pleased to have a new brother or sister. How far gone are you?
ELAINE:	About 14 weeks. It's due at the end of August – Gordon's birthday, in fact, would you believe?
MARIA:	*(hugs Elaine)* I'm so pleased for you, Elaine. *(she turns away to get coffee so* ELAINE *can't see the tears in her eyes)*

[back in the dining room]

JONATHAN:	So what are those two gossiping about, do you suppose? Probably us!
GORDON:	Well, Elaine might be telling Maria our news.
JONATHAN:	What news is that, then?
GORDON:	Well, Elaine's pregnant again. *(excited)* We're having another baby!
JONATHAN:	Oh, my commiserations to you, mate! More nappies and sleepless nights!
GORDON:	Jon!
JONATHAN:	No, sorry, mate. Congratulations, I know you've been wanting this for a while, haven't you?
GORDON:	Yes, the family just didn't feel complete without a brother or sister for William.

[back in the kitchen]

ELAINE:	Maria, are you OK?
MARIA:	Yes, I'm fine, really.
ELAINE:	*(turning her round to face her)* No, you're not. What's the matter?
MARIA:	*(wiping away a tear)* I guess I'm just happy for you.
ELAINE:	Yes, you look it!
MARIA:	Oh, I'm sorry, Elaine. I am happy for you, I am really, It's just …
ELAINE:	Just what?

MARIA:	Oh, I don't know. I just feel a bit envious of you, I suppose.
ELAINE:	Envious of me? You're joking! You with your partnership and company Mercedes. You with your holidays in Barbados and me with a week in Bournemouth! I don't think so!
MARIA:	No, envious of this *(puts her hand on Elaine's tummy)*.
ELAINE:	Of the baby? But you don't want children!

[back in the dining room]

JONATHAN:	What do you mean, didn't feel complete? You don't need children to feel complete, mate. Look at Maria and me, we have a wonderful relationship without kids.
GORDON:	No, I know, Jon. Sorry, I didn't mean it like that. It's just that Elaine and I really wanted another baby. Children are something we've always wanted. I know you and Maria feel differently about that. You want different things out of life.
JONATHAN:	Yes, this house isn't exactly conducive to kids, is it! When I designed it, I wasn't thinking about dangerous ledges and slippery floors – I was thinking about what Maria and I wanted.
GORDON:	And I must say, Jon, it really is beautiful – you're a lucky guy.
JONATHAN:	I know. I have a great job, wonderful home and beautiful wife. What more could a man ask for?

[GORDON is about to answer then thinks better of it.]

[back in the kitchen]

MARIA:	*(quietly)* Didn't.
ELAINE:	Pardon?
MARIA:	Didn't want children.
ELAINE:	What? You've changed your mind?
MARIA:	Yes, I suppose I have.
ELAINE:	But you are the one person I thought didn't have a maternal bone in her body. For as long as I've known you, you've never wanted children.

MARIA:	I know.
ELAINE:	Too selfish, you always said you were. Wanted a career, you said. No time for babies.
MARIA:	I know.
ELAINE:	So what's changed?
MARIA:	Me, I suppose.

[back in the dining room]

GORDON:	Have you never wanted kids, Jon?
JONATHAN:	No, never.
GORDON:	And Maria – has she never felt slightly broody?
JONATHAN:	No. When we first met, it was one of the first things we talked about, actually. Both of us wanted the same things out of life. Successful careers and a high standard of living. Babies just weren't on the agenda. And here we are, eleven years on, having done exactly what we wanted. Quite an achievement, really.
GORDON:	And you feel fulfilled?
JONATHAN:	Grief, that's a bit of a heavy question for this time of night! It must be the wine!
GORDON:	Well, do you?
JONATHAN:	Sure. I've built up the business enough to allow me lots of time off for golf and the gym. That's why I could run rings around you!
GORDON:	Oh yes, but how well can you name the characters in *The Tweenies (or appropriate children's programme)*?
JONATHAN:	I rest my case!

[back in the kitchen]

| ELAINE: | But I thought you were really happy with your life as it was. You and Jon seem to have such a great relationship, and you live the life of Riley! |

MARIA: I know. It's not that I'm unhappy, 'cos I'm not. I love Jon and I love my life. It's just that somehow it's not enough. Over the last year or so I've been thinking to myself, what now? I've succeeded with all the challenges I've set myself and still I don't feel satisfied.

ELAINE: But a baby isn't necessarily the answer.

MARIA: I know that, I'm not saying it is. It's just that recently I've been feeling that I'd like to build a family with Jon, not just an empire.

[in the dining room]

GORDON: Well, I'm glad you feel totally satisfied with life, Jon. You should bottle that feeling and sell it. You'd make a fortune.

JONATHAN: Don't get me wrong, Gordon. I don't mean to sound arrogant. I don't think for one minute I've got it all right. In fact, there are many occasions when I wonder if this is all there is to life, but then I get in the Porsche and know I've found heaven! Anyway, where are the girls with coffee? *(shouting into the kitchen)* Come on, Maria. Have you been to Kenya to pick the beans yourself? We're dying of thirst in here!

[in the kitchen]

ELAINE: Does Jonathan know?

MARIA: No. *(calling to Jon)* Coming!

ELAINE: You have to tell him.

MARIA: No, I don't. *(calling to Jon)* Darling, can you get the port? *(to Elaine)* We made an agreement when we got married. No children. I can't go back on that now – it wouldn't be fair.

[They walk back across to dining room with tray of drinks and sit back down]

MARIA: *(feigning brightness)* Sorry about that. Coffee's up. Did you get the port? Good. Pass it round then – only to the left!

GORDON: Did you tell Maria our news, darling?

ELAINE:	Yes I did. *(pointedly)* What do you think, Jon?
JONATHAN:	I think it's wonderful news. Congratulations, Elaine. Children are great when they're someone else's, aren't they, darling?
MARIA:	*(quietly)* Yes, I suppose so.
JONATHAN:	You can play with them and then give them back when they start crying – that's the best deal, I reckon. I mean, fancy trying to play a round of golf after you've been up half the night. I mean it would put you right off your stroke!
MARIA:	*(quietly)* You could just give up golf.
JONATHAN:	Sorry?
MARIA:	Nothing. Come on, Gordon. You're hogging the port.
ELAINE:	*(pursuing the point)* Have you never wanted children, Jon?
JONATHAN:	What is this? Gordon's just asked me the same question. You know Maria and I don't want a family. We're very pleased for you two, but we made a decision a long time ago.
ELAINE:	And you're still happy to stick by that decision, are you, even though you made it over ten years ago?
JONATHAN:	Yes, why?
ELAINE:	And Maria, is she still happy not to have children?
JONATHAN:	Of course she is. She's the senior partner in Brandon Phillips – she's hardly got time for a baby now, have you, love?
MARIA:	Well ...
JONATHAN:	See!
ELAINE:	I didn't hear her agreeing with you!
MARIA:	*(warningly)* Elaine!
JONATHAN:	I think I know my wife well enough to know.
ELAINE:	I'm not so sure.
GORDON:	Elaine, I really think ...
JONATHAN:	No, I'm interested. Elaine obviously knows my wife's opinions on having babies better than I do – I'd like to hear what she has to say.

ELAINE:	Maria?
MARIA:	I'm not sure this is the right time, Elaine.
JONATHAN:	Right time for what?
MARIA:	Well …
JONATHAN:	Well what? Is she right? Am I wrong about this? If I am I need to know.
MARIA:	Well, it's just that – Elaine being pregnant and everything – *(blurting out)* I think I'm a bit broody.
JONATHAN:	*(this is the last thing he was expecting her to say)* You? Broody? I never thought I'd hear you say that!
ELAINE:	Yes, well, maybe you just don't listen.
GORDON AND MARIA TOGETHER:	Elaine!
JONATHAN:	*(not really listening to* ELAINE *and now feeling quite perturbed)* But I don't understand, Maria. We agreed when we first met – neither of us wanted children.
MARIA:	I know, Jon. It's my fault. I was only 20 then and a student. I've changed.
JONATHAN:	Well, I don't quite know what to say. This is a bit of a bombshell for my birthday, isn't it?
GORDON:	I'm sorry, Jon. This is our fault, we shouldn't have brought the subject up. It's just that we're so excited.
ELAINE:	Yes, I'm sorry. I shouldn't have pushed things. Come on, Gordon. We should be going anyway – I told the babysitter eleven o'clock.

[They get up.]

ELAINE:	Thanks for a lovely evening. I'll ring you tomorrow, Maria.
GORDON:	Bye, you two. See you soon

[They exit.]

MARIA: *(getting up)* Well, I suppose I should start clearing this away.

[Jon pulls her back down.]

JONATHAN: No, Maria, we need to talk about this. Are you serious? Do you really want a baby?

MARIA: I don't want to argue about it, Jonathan. There's nothing I can do about it.

JONATHAN: But you were the one who was always so adamant. More so than me, in fact.

MARIA: I know, I know.

JONATHAN: Well, this changes everything! I think we'd better make another pot of coffee. We've got a lot of talking to do.

[They exit as lights fade.]

Who'd Be a Mother?

Nicki Matthews

This monologue is a fly-on-the-wall observation of a scene in a 'normal' family home somewhere between teatime and bedtime. Mum Lisa is trying to keep her head above water when all her children around her are doing their best to give her a nervous breakdown!

Lisa is on the telephone to her friend Jill, who has called to see how she is, and the dialogue switches from that conversation to words with Lisa's children, who we never see but can clearly imagine.

This sketch was inspired by the many conversations I have attempted to have with my sister on the phone, regularly punctuated with interruptions from her three wonderful little boys.

Anyone with their own children or close to those who do will identify with this sketch, which illustrates very clearly a young woman whose life has been completely taken over by her children, although she perhaps is not aware of it.

👤	👤	🕐
1	0	5 minutes

Other themes

Over-work

Characters

LISA: Rather tired and fractious mother, aged roughly 35, who loves children and family life dearly but doesn't realise how they are taking over her life

Costumes

General comfort clothes such as a leisure or track suit, with perhaps an apron and probably with a stain on the shoulder from the baby. No make-up, hair scraped into a pony tail if possible.

All you need

❏ Cordless 'walk around' telephone
❏ Sound effects: telephone ringing, loud music

Special notes: As we only hear one side of this conversation, the actress playing the part of Lisa must be sure to leave short silences to indicate either that Jill is speaking at the other end of the phone or that her children are replying to her. To help with this, we have marked spaces in the script to enable you to pause.

[Lights fade up and a telephone is heard ringing from somewhere on set. LISA enters looking fraught and trying to find the telephone handset. Eventually she finds it in her pocket; this allows you to use a real mobile phone and puts Lisa in control of switching the sound off rather than the sound team!]

LISA: (*answering phone*) Hello … Oh, hi Jill, how are you? … Good … Yes, I'm fine, thanks. I'm so sorry I haven't rung you for ages, things have just been so frantic.

(*suddenly notices child and leaps to the left as if she is looking through to the kitchen*) Tom, Tom, leave that alone … I don't care if you like it better that colour, Daddy likes to wear white shirts for work.

(*back to phone*) Sorry, Jill, you were saying …? Really! Since when?

(*looking up in front of her*) John, don't kick that football in here! How many times do I have to tell you? If you want to play football, go outside (*shouting after him*) but make sure you've done your homework first – John! John! Oh, never mind!

(*back to phone*) Sorry, I didn't quite catch that … That long! Well you'd never have guessed, would you?

(*sees* TOM *in the kitchen again*) TOM! Don't give that to the baby! … She doesn't like it! She crying … It's Rex's toy and is probably filthy dirty … Because he's a dog … Because dogs are animals and animals are dirty (*realising she might be losing the argument*) … I know he doesn't look dirty but he is … Because he rolls around the garden and eats all sorts of rubbish, that's why! … Because, because, just because. Rex, down! (*slapping her side to try and stop the dog jumping up*) Now see what you've done! REX! Give him back his toy, go on. Rex, no! … Now he didn't hurt you that much, did he … no, don't pull his tail or he will hurt you. (*shouting after him*) No, don't chase him, Tom. Oh, I give up!

[loud music starts playing]

(back to phone) So, what did Jack say? No! Really? I can't believe …

(looking up and shouting over the music) Katie, will you turn that music down! …

(to phone) … that he'd react like that.

(shouting upstairs) Katie! *(music stops)* Thank you.

(to phone) Teenage daughters! Who'd have 'em?

Mind you, I can't imagine what …

(looks up to see daughter) What on earth are you wearing, young lady? My top I think, and if that piece of material was sold as a skirt the shop should be done under the Trade Descriptions Act! That wouldn't even be described as a mini on Barbie! You go straight back up those stairs and change please – you're not going anywhere dressed like that!

(back to phone) Pardon? No, no really, you haven't got me at a bad time at all. I'm glad you rang, actually. I …

(notices TOM *on the floor in front of her)* Tom, what have you done with that crayon? You didn't just post it into the video slot did you? … Oh Thomas, not again! I've only just managed to retrieve the last bit of potato waffle from the mechanism. You are a pain!

(back to phone) Sorry, Jill. Got any suggestions for removing foreign objects from sensitive pieces of equipment! … Oh really? Does that work? … Oh great, I'll give it a go.

*(*KATIE *appears again)* That's much better … What, now? Well, you haven't had tea yet! …. Of course you need to eat! Look, do me a favour, stick those sausages under the grill for me and I'll drive you over there in a while. Thanks, love.

(to phone) Sorry, Jill, what was I saying?

(looking to her right) John, that ball nearly came through the window! Will you please be careful!

(to phone) Oh yes, I've been meaning to ring you actually …

(to TOM on floor in front of her) Thomas! Will you please stop doing that!

(to phone) Me?

(to the left) Katie, those sausages are burning and I think Sophie needs changing. Would you nip upstairs and get me a nappy please?

(to phone) No, not much, really.

(to TOM) Thomas, I won't tell you again. Do you want to go up to your room?

(to phone) Same as usual, only …

(to right) John! Once more and I'm confiscating that ball!

(to phone) One thing I have been meaning to tell you …

(to the left) Katie, the sausages! Well, put the magazine down, and have you got me a nappy yet?

(to phone) … but haven't got round to …

(to baby in baby voice) I'll be there in a minute, Sophie darling.

(to phone) … never seem to have the time …

(to front) Thomas!

(to phone) Yes, my news is …

(to right) John!

(to phone) Wonderful news, actually. I'm pregnant again!

[Blackout]

Millennium Newsdesk: Headline 'Pregnant Man'

Alison Wright, David Robinson, Nicki Matthews, Mandy Watsham

This sketch features a newsreader presenting a news report from the year 2034. Looking into the future, it takes a comical look at what we might expect to see in years to come, including a theme park in the grounds of Buckingham Palace – now owned by Richard Branson – and the celebrations of the late Queen's mother's 135th birthday. (This headline should be omitted if inappropriate.)

It also includes the breaking story of Mr Jacobs, the very first pregnant man. Speaking to Mr Jacobs in the studio, the female newscaster is very interested to find out just how he is coping with the rigours of pregnancy.

This sketch is not meant to be taken seriously other than to illustrate just how quickly things change. It can be used to great effect as a preamble to a talk or section about the constancy of God.

👤	👤	🕐
1	1	4 minutes

Other themes

The future

Characters

NEWSREADER: BBC-style voice
PREGNANT MAN: From the East End of London, with an obvious 'bump'

Costumes

NEWSREADER: Smart suit
PREGNANT MAN: Dungarees or similar maternity wear with cushion placed to
                give appearance of eight months pregnancy

All you need

❏ Desk and chair for newsreader
❏ Parenting magazine
❏ Tape of news theme, with Big Ben chime

[Music intro]

NEWSREADER: Good evening. Welcome to the BBC Millennium Newsdesk on 25 November 2034.

The headlines tonight: Richard Branson's latest plans for Buckingham Palace *(sound effect: bong!)*; who's in and who's out in this year's Beckham Cultural Awards *(sound effect: bong!)*; and tonight's main story – he's six foot two, works out in the gym, and he is eight months pregnant. Yes, Trevor Jacobs from east London is preparing for the birth of his baby next month. I, and indeed all the other women at the Millennium Newsdesk, were extremely interested to hear how he was coping. Mr Jacobs joins me now in the studio.

[Enter MR JACOBS with a bit of a waddle]

Good evening, Mr Jacobs, and thank you for joining me this evening. First, let me ask you: do you know what it is yet?

MR JACOBS: Yes, the wife and I decided we wanted to know what it is. It's on page 12, catalogue number 1056 – boy, blond hair, blue eyes, suitable to the name of Adrian and likely to be good at rugby. Cor, football more like, if this kicking is anything to go by.

NEWSREADER: So how are you coping?

MR JACOBS: Well, I haven't been sleeping too well. In fact, haven't had a wink this last week. It's been so hot in bed! I can't fit into any of my clothes any more. And my ankles have swollen up like balloons. I've been to see the doctor, and she just smiled and said, 'The worst is yet to come, Mr Jacobs, the worst is yet to come.' She seemed to enjoy telling me that, actually.

NEWSREADER: And your wife, how does she feel about it all?

MR JACOBS: Well, of course, she's got no idea what I'm going through! She just paces infuriatingly up and down the lounge chewing on a big chunk of chocolate. She keeps offering me endless cups of tea because I happened to mention a couple of weeks ago that I couldn't face another cup of coffee. She's bought me a whole case of cocktail pickled onions from the cash and carry because I had a little craving for them last week, and every evening she pops down the pub with the girls from work to discuss – and I quote – 'things I wouldn't understand'!

NEWSREADER: Does she plan to be there at the birth?

MR JACOBS: Absolutely! She insists on being there, with the video camera Great-Uncle Harry gave us for Christmas on her shoulder. I've told her, I have, she can make sure she stays at the top end – I mean, people don't want to see that type of thing on their TV screens, do they?

NEWSREADER: But you must accept, Mr Jacobs, there's bound to be media interest – I mean, you'll be the first man ever to give birth.

MR JACOBS: I know, I know. I'll be making history when I do give birth … *(thinking)* I haven't quite worked out how I'm going to do it yet … *(thinking and wincing)* I don't like to think about it for too long!

NEWSREADER: You must have been preparing for it, though?

MR JACOBS: Oh yes. I've read a few magazines, watched some videos, been to ante-natal a few times and wandered around Mothercare. And, to be honest, I'm not sure what all the fuss is about. There doesn't seem to be too much to it. It seems to me, all these women do is sweat and shout a lot, and there it is. I've been doing that for years!

NEWSREADER: *(hurriedly interrupting)* Thank you, Mr Jacobs.

[MR JACOBS smiles, looking rather bemused and mouths to an imaginary studio manager, 'Can I go now?' He obviously doesn't hear the reply and so wanders off anyway.]

NEWSREADER: *(trying to ignore him, stares resolutely into the camera)* Now to our other main stories this evening: the 84-year-old multi-billionaire Richard Branson, recently named the world's richest man following the collapse of Bill Gates' billion-dollar empire, completed his purchase of Buckingham Palace today. Branson, who reportedly set up a business partnership with King William in the early 2020s, was quoted as saying, 'I have great plans for the Palace.' Branson's plans will include opening up the Palace to the public and making rooms available for private hire – guests can have daily use of the throne. He hopes to make the Palace the number one venue for European society weddings. Still to come will be the building of a billion-pound Euro theme park in the grounds. (However, these plans will have to wait until early next year after the late Queen's mother has celebrated her 135th birthday at the Palace.) At present, Mr Branson is relaxing in his holiday home, the Taj Mahal.

The latest writer to come under the axe is William Shakespeare, heralded in the last century as 'Man of the Millennium'. Shakespeare has been withdrawn from all websites and education curricula for being sexist, racist and politically incorrect. This news comes in the week that three writers have been honoured at this year's Beckham Awards for outstanding contributions to British culture. Literature prizes were awarded to three great classical writers, Thomas Hardy, Enid Blyton, and the late great twentieth-century literary genius, Jackie Collins. Narrowly missing success were Jilly Cooper and the indomitable Barbara Cartland.

The lifetime achievement award was once again given to Lord Cliff Richard for his sheer staying power. The 94-year-old singer said that to celebrate winning the trophy, he would be playing the lead in a new musical in the West End based on the story of Peter Pan.

That's all from this edition of Millennium Newsdesk. Join us again tomorrow, when we'll bring you the latest update on the Pregnant Man. I'm sure there'll be an opening for him somewhere! Good night. *(freeze smile)*

[Theme music outro]

Hats

Nicki Matthews

This is a fast-moving monologue illustrating how many job roles the average wife and mother fulfils in a normal day.

The sketch is performed on a blank stage, with only a table centre stage, and the action takes place during a 'typical' weekday evening. As she takes on the different roles within the family, Emma changes her position and uses different hats to illustrate the variety of roles. From chauffeur to cook and from maid to lover, we observe how versatile a mother has to be and the demands this makes on her life.

This sketch will undoubtedly appeal to women, as they will immediately identify with Emma, but may also help men understand the pressures on women today.

🧍‍♀️	🧍	🕐
1	0	5 minutes

Other themes

Family life, Mother's Day

Characters

EMMA: A thirty-something wife and mother who is completely programmed into carrying out the roles her husband and children expect of her

Costumes

All black, to provide a neutral palate on which to add the following:

All you need

❏ Chauffeur's cap
❏ Chef's hat
❏ Teacher's mortar board
❏ Maid's lacy mob cap
❏ Nurse's cap
❏ Waitress's white apron
❏ Cleaner's 'Hilda' headscarf
❏ Shrink's white coat/clipboard
❏ PA's glasses/notepad
❏ Lover's jewellery and rose
❏ Table, centre stage
❏ Sound effect of telephone ringing
❏ Pen and piece of paper that looks like a questionnaire

[The scene is set with a table in the centre upon which are all the different hats. EMMA is seated on the table, wearing the chauffeur's cap and pretending to drive. She takes all roles.]

CHAUFFEUR: Hello, girls, good day at school? Oh dear, Emily. Have you got a plaster on it? And did Mr Johnston like your project, Jenny? Oh, well done, B+! Daddy will be impressed.

[They have arrived home; EMMA mimes parking the car, gets out and changes hats; faces front.]

TEACHER: Right, homework first, please. What have you got? Maths and English. Right, get your books out and then we'll have tea – who wants fish fingers and chips?

[turns to face right and changes hat]

CHEF: Tea's nearly ready! Have you finished?

[turns to face front again and changes hat]

TEACHER: Spell 'message' for me, then, Jenny. *(Listens)* Well done. And let's hear your two times table, Emily *(listens)*.

[turns to face left and changes hat]

MAID: Tea's ready. Oh, good timing, Luke – come on, sit down and have your tea before you do your homework. How was football practice?

[turns to face front and changes hat]

NURSE: Oh dear, that does look nasty. Did you put ice on it? Look, sit down there and I'll find something to try and take the swelling down a bit.

[telephone rings – EMMA turns to face right, puts on glasses and picks up phone]

PA: Hello. No, I'm sorry, he's not available at the moment. Can I take a message? Yes, yes, I'm sure that'll be fine. I'll let him know and if it's a problem he'll give you a call back. OK. Thanks, Bye.

[turns to face front and changes hat]

MAID: Right, have you finished? *(mimes collecting up plates)* Good. OK, you two, up to the bath please. Luke, what homework have you got? PSE? What's that all about, then? Oh right, well, if you need any help I'll be in the lounge – the dust on the TV is so thick I could draw a picture in it.

[turns to face left and changes hat]

CLEANER: *(dusting)* 5.30 p.m. OK. Half an hour until James gets home. Spaghetti bolognaise tonight, I think.

[turns to face right and changes hat]

CHEF: Right, that should be ready in 25 minutes. Just time to read the girls a story and check on Luke's homework.

[turns to face front, puts on white coat and holds clipboard]

SHRINK: Hello, darling. How was your day? Really? Oh dear. Do you want to tell me about it? I'm sure it wasn't that bad.. Come on, darling, open up to me. Let it all out and you'll feel much better.

[turns to face left and puts on white apron]

WAITRESS: *(putting plate on table)* Dinner's ready, darling. Would you like parmesan or black pepper? Glass of wine? Red or white? Enjoy your meal!

[turns to face right and puts on hat]

TEACHER: Well, you should have started this essay earlier, shouldn't you!
Ask Miss Jones if you can have an extension till Monday and I'll
help you at the weekend.

[turns to face left and changes hat]

MAID: Did you enjoy that? Good. Any dessert? OK, I'll wash up and join
you in the lounge in a few minutes. Go on, I think the news is on.

[turns to face right and changes hat]

CHAUFFEUR: I'll be back in a few minutes, James. I forgot it's Scouts tonight,
and I'm doing the first run. I'll see you later. You don't need to
worry about the girls, they're tucked up in bed.

[turns to face front and changes hat]

MAID: I'm back. Do you want a cup of coffee? By the way –

[turns to face left and puts on glasses]

PA: David rang earlier and asked if you could make breakfast next
Wednesday instead of Tuesday. I said to assume it's OK unless
you ring. Good.

[turns to face right with jewellery and rose; then, slightly slower]

LOVER: So, did you miss me today? I know you've had a rough day. Do
you want me to massage your shoulders? An early night? Yes,
why not. You go on up. Why don't you run a bath? I'll join you in
a minute. I've just got to finish this shoppers' survey, otherwise I
won't get all those money-off vouchers. The closing date's
Saturday so I need to get it in the post tomorrow. I started it
ages ago, but for some reason I haven't got round to finishing it.

[sits on the table with no hats or accessories]

Right *(checking off things she has already ticked)* Tesco, *Daily Mail*, Renault, Persil, Weetabix. Oh, I should think twice a year *(filling these details in)*. Name, address, age 30 to 40. Occupation? Oh, I don't know, really. Um. Well, I suppose it's just housewife.

[Blackout]

CHAPTER 11

all work and no play makes …

Work and leisure

The world in which we live continues to get more and more pressurised, with more time spent working and less time relaxing.

This section includes three songs and four sketches based on the subjects of work and leisure – one of the hot subjects of the twenty-first century.

So if you're looking for a song to illustrate pure relaxation or a sketch about queuing in the supermarket – look no further!

SONGS

❏   Purrfect Day
❏   Stop This Ride
❏   The Clock Is Ticking

SCRIPTS

Anyone for Badminton?
Monologue by Caroline who is playing badminton in the church hall as a result of her husband's attempts to get her into the building. A look at how those outside the church view Christianity.

Mind the Gap
Four people on the Tube assess each other by what they look like and how they expect others to be.

The Christmas Bash
Liz and Andrew are in the car on the way to the company Christmas bash. Andrew is obviously not keen on going, and we only find out the real reason for this right at the end of the sketch: at this point there are two alternative endings.

Hurry Sickness
A customer in a local supermarket is held up in the queue and displays all signs of having 'hurry sickness' – that is, no patience at all!

Purrfect Day

Words and music by Mandy Watsham

This is a fun, light jazz, up-tempo song with lots of character. 'Purrfect Day' has a real twist in the tail! The song sings about being lazy and spending relaxing days in the sun, and could in fact be talking about any of us. However, as the last part of the song unfolds, the culprit of the piece is revealed to be, in fact, a cat!

It's a fun, nonsense type of song which could be great as an opener or an ice-breaker for programmes based on the themes of leisure, idleness, work or relaxation.

As written, the song works very well with three-part harmony throughout, and unison where no other part is written. However, it can work just as well sung as a solo with lots of performance, zest and character.

The introduction and verses 1 and 2 start very slowly, to illustrate the lazy feel of the piece. Verse 1 should be played just by the bass, giving an 'empty' feel. For verse 2 a guitar playing chords and sustained keyboard chords could be added. The tempo picks up on the second time bar on the word 'attitude', with a crescendo and dramatic increase of pace.

As the song progresses, the chord structure remains the same, with different inversions to give the impression that the price is getting higher and higher. After that frenzied vocal activity, the band or pianist can have a field day playing an instrumental version the second time through the up-tempo section.

At the end of the instrumental, it goes right back to the beginning of the piece, to the slow tempo of the start with the bass notes plodding out the rhythm and chords from the guitar and keyboard, as for verse 2. Verse 3 finishes the song as it reveals the story, and as long as diction is good and the audience have been listening, they should get the drift of the sultry, then frenzied performance that they have just witnessed.

Purrfect Day

Jazzy, with character ♩ = c.96

1. Laz-ing on a sun-ny Sun-day af-ter-noon, sit-ting a-round with not___
2. Tak-ing it___ ea-sy, . . .
3. Id-ling on a steam-y . . .

much to do,___ stretch-ing out___ long___ and___ feel-ing fine,

yawn-ing slow-ly, so di-vine. at-ti-tude.___

Sun up in morn - ing   till sun goes down,   I live a life of
(2nd time instrumental)

ease,   wake him with kiss - es   to start the day,

then things will go   my   way.   I make an en - trance

with dig-ni - ty,   real dig-ni-fied and   sure.   Tread si-lent-ly to

show lots of style   as   I take   the   floor.

Life is mys-ter - ious,   don't you a-gree?   Suits my cu - ri - o - si -

- ty.   No - bo - dy owns   me,   I suit my-self,

I come and go   as I   please.

Verse 1
Lazing on a sunny Sunday afternoon,
sitting around with not much to do,
stretching out long and feeling fine,
yawning slowly, so divine.

Verse 2
Taking it easy, showing great repose,
watching the world go by with eyes still closed,
trust my intuition, I ain't nobody's fool,
live life with my attitude.

Sun up in morning till sun goes down,
I live a life of ease,
wake him with kisses to start the day,
then things will go my way.
I make an entrance with dignity,
real dignified and sure.
Tread silently to show lots of style
as I take the floor.
Life is mysterious, don't you agree?
Suits my curiosity.
Nobody owns me, I suit myself,
I come and go as I please.

Verse 3
Idling on a steamy Sunday lazily,
covered with a cloak of sensuality,
contentment oozing out from every single paw,
I may purr, but watch my claw!

Stop This Ride

Words and music by Mandy Watsham

This is a busy, bright, bustling song, the feel of which indicates the general theme of the piece – busy-ness. Where does the time go? Why are there not enough hours in the day? What are our priorities?

The world today is a very different place to that of fifty years ago, and at times it can feel as if we're on a roller-coaster ride that we just can't get off. Sometimes it feels as if life, with its schedules and demands, is controlling us, and we have the general despairing feeling of being utterly powerless.

As the song moves along at a fair lick, good diction is important to ensure that the frenzied theme and nature of the song is put across and heard. The piece opens with eight bars of fast-moving quavers, and the song commences with the chorus.

The verses maintain the pace throughout, and the words talk about trying to cram everything into a life with precious little room for manoeuvre anyway. The end of the verse states clearly that though life may be busy 'the message I'm giving is that this isn't living'.

It continues by going into the bridge: 'When will this all end. I'm living like it's twenty miles a minute. And when it's gone what's left to burn but remnants of the embers of regrets'.

The song ends by simply stating 'Don't leave the embers of regrets'.

Stop This Ride

Stop this ride I ___ wan - na get off, ___ rest ___ ___ in - side ___ is ___ what I do not. ___ End - less line – when will it all end? ___ Just ___ in time ___ be - fore I go in - sane?

1. Meet - ings ga - lore, dead - lines by the score,   my head's bu - sy spin-ning by the
2. Night times get la - ter . . .

weight that it's gi - ven.   Keep-ing in trim, some-thing else to fit in,__ the

mes-sage I'm giv - ing   is that   this is - n't liv - ing, yeah.__

1 & 2. When will this__ all__ end?_____ I'm____ liv - ing like__ it's
3.   *Instrumental*
4. When will this__ all__ end?_____ There   comes a time_ when

(1.2.) twen-ty   miles   a min - ute. And when it's   gone,_____ what's
(4.) you de - serve   to live._____ A pre-cious   life,_____ the

left_ to burn?   But rem-nants_ of__ the em - bers of__ re -

piano as intro

- grets?   - grets?

CODA

time‿ to breathe and take in what's a‿round‿ you. Don't let your life‿

‿ con‿sume‿ and break your soul,_____ don't leave the em - bers of‿

‿ re‿grets,_____ don't leave the em - bers of___

‿ re‿grets,_____ don't leave the em - bers of_____ re‿grets.

Chorus
Stop this ride I wanna get off,
rest inside is what I do not.
Endless line – when will it all end?
Just in time before I go insane?

Verse 1
Meetings galore, deadlines by the score,
my head's busy spinning by the weight that it's given.
Keeping in trim, something else to fit in,
the message I'm giving is that this isn't living, yeah.

Bridge
When will this all end?
I'm living like it's twenty miles a minute.
And when it's gone,
What's left to burn?
But remnants of the embers of regrets?

Chorus

Verse 2
Night times get later, mornings seem earlier,
the candle's still burning yet it's four in the morning.
The lesson of love is to give all you've got,
the rate that I'm learning I'll never start turning around.

Bridge

Instrumental Bridge

Bridge into coda
When will this all end?
There comes a time when you deserve to live.
A precious life, the time to breathe and take in what's around you.
Don't let your life consume and break your soul,
don't leave the embers of regrets.

Don't leave the embers of regrets,
don't leave the embers of regrets.

The Clock Is Ticking

Words and music by Mandy Watsham

For Pop

This song is a fairly fast-moving piece that has contrasting styles almost like three different movements contained in one musical piece.

The subject matter talks broadly about time and the alarming rate at which it passes the older we get.

Verse 1 says, 'Life moves so fast, childhood dreams fade. Pictures and memories still remain. Yesterday's gone. Where did the days go? Time keeps on rolling along.' Verse 2 goes on to talk about the endless uncomplicated feeling of childhood.

The chorus needs to have a 16 feel from the drums to emphasise the speed at which the years go by: 'Just 'cos the clock keeps on ticking doesn't mean that I have changed. I feel the same deep inside despite the rolling of the years.'

The last part of the chorus goes into smoother feel now, with the main beats pushed on the bass drum – 'Love walks in the room you fill my heart with pride, I will go on needing you until the day I die.'

The song continues in these contrasting styles until the challenge of the second chorus: 'the times we spend in these Shadowlands is minimal at best' (C.S. Lewis).

The end of the piece finishes with a melodic, poignant last movement, which simply states, 'Yes, the child has grown but still the girl/boy remains inside – the shell may change still my heart remains for ever by your side.' And then the final challenge: 'The present only is our time, a gift that's ours to share. Let's start today. Tomorrow may be too late.'

The message of the song is simply that all of us should make the effort to spend precious quality time with the people we care about and have the privilege of being on this earth with . Our time in these Shadowlands is short, and tomorrow, regretfully, may be too late.

The Clock Is Ticking

1. Life moves so fast, child - hood dreams fade, pic - tures and
2. When I was young . . .
3. Sea - sons may come . . .

mem - 'ries still re - main.＿ Yes - ter - day's gone. Where did the＿ days

go? Time keeps on roll - ing＿ a - long.＿＿＿ - long.＿＿＿

Just 'cos the clock keeps on tick - ing does - n't mean that I＿ have changed,

Verse 1

Life moves so fast, childhood dreams fade,
pictures and mem'ries still remain.
Yesterday's gone. Where did the days go?
Time keeps on rolling along.

Verse 2

When I was young, dreams meant so much,
I was content to ride my luck.
Life was uncluttered, days stretched like years,
time kept on rolling along.

Just 'cos the clock keeps on ticking doesn't mean that I have changed,
I feel the same deep inside despite the rolling of the years.
I won't forget when my grandma told me she still felt sixteen years old,
age can't defy what we feel inside, despite our limbs trying to tell us so.

Love walks in the room, you fill my heart with pride.
I will go on needing you until the day I die.

Verse 3

Seasons they come, seasons they go.
No-one knows what happens next.
Yesterday's gone. Where did the days go?
Time keeps on rolling along.

Just 'cos the clock keeps on ticking doesn't mean that I have changed,
I feel the same deep inside despite the rolling of the years.
The time we spend in these Shadowlands is minimal at best,
So while we've got it spare I'd like to spend some time with you.

Love walks in the room, you fill my heart with pride,
You gave me love and you taught me how to fly.
Yes, the child has grown but still the girl remains inside,
the shell may change still my heart remains
forever by your side.

The present only is our time, a gift that's ours to share,
let's start today,
tomorrow may be too late.

Yes, the child has grown but still the girl remains inside,
the shell may change still my heart remains
forever by your side.
The present only is our time, a gift that's ours to share,
let's start today,
tomorrow may be too late,
too late,
tomorrow may be too late.

Anyone for Badminton?

Tim Goodwright, adapted by Nicki Matthews

This monologue takes a look at how those outside the church view Christianity. All too often, people have misconceptions about what church is really like. This sketch highlights some of these preconceived ideas as we hear Caroline's thoughts on the subject while she plays badminton in the church hall.

Jeff and Caroline are married. Jeff goes to church, Caroline doesn't. The sketch opens as they are talking by the door; Caroline is preparing to play a game of badminton. From her comments, we can recognise that she clearly believes church has nothing relevant to offer her at all, although she doesn't mind her husband attending as long as he doesn't try preaching to her. It soon becomes obvious that Jeff is trying to get Caroline over the threshold of the church, and if he can't get her to a service he'll at least get her there with her badminton racket!

Judy is a third person, unseen, who plays from the audience: so, in effect, Caroline talks to the audience. The piece should be performed like a telephone conversation, allowing time for Judy to speak. Make sure every stroke is played and every move is planned, otherwise you will get totally confused!

🧍‍♀️	🧍	⏱️
1	0	5 minutes

Other themes

Marriage, evangelism

Characters

CAROLINE: A young mother with pre-conceived ideas about the church

Costumes

Sportswear

All you need

❏ Badminton racket
❏ Shuttlecocks
❏ Sports bag

[CAROLINE arrives and is talking to her unseen husband, who is just outside the door. She is obviously irritated with him.]

CAROLINE: Yes, Jeff, I'll be fine. Yes, Jeff, I know where the toilets are. No, Jeff, I don't need a lift home – Judy and I will probably walk – it's a nice evening, isn't it. OK. I think I can hear the twins whinging in the car, you'd better go. Thanks. Bye.

(turning to the game) Right, shall we skip the knock around and go straight in? Lovely. Are you all right up that end? We can always change later …

[plays a couple of shots]

What, Jeff? No, he's looking after the twins tonight.

[she plays; collects shuttlecocks from the net, etc., as she speaks]

Why play here? I ask myself the same question. It was Jeff's idea. He comes to church here and they're doing something called a mission. It's a Billy Graham kind of thing. I'm not sure – I think the idea is to make the church more *(bends knees to squat position as if warming up)* down to earth – they do a Mums and Toddlers group and coffee mornings and stuff, and, of course, make this hall available for anyone who wants to use it. I don't know why they bother …

Well, apparently, they want more people to come to the church – well, it's hard enough booking this hall in the first place. There's dance class, drama club and goodness knows what else … anyway, so Jeff suggested playing badminton here.

Well, it's hardly the Harbour Club, is it? But anything to get out of the house.

[comes to the net and reluctantly admits …]

You see, Jeff doesn't like me going to the gym any more. Well, not since he found out the aerobic classes were mixed and that it was more likely that my leotard would cause the men to overheat than the exercises themselves! He reckons I wasn't behaving as a happily married mother of twins should.

[she goes to play but there is a blackout]

> Blast! The meter's run out – have you got any 50ps, Judy? I forgot to get some. Brilliant – well, the meter's in the men's toilet. Well, there's not going to be anyone in there now!

[she shouts as JUDY is directed where to go]

> Keep going till you find the wall – are you there? Yes, that would be the wall. Lovely. Now go right and you'll find a doorway. Go through and down the corridor and the meter is behind the door.
>
> Stupid system. Don't put more than 50p in – you'll end up paying for someone else's electricity!

[lights on]

> That's got them – well done, Jude. But as I say, it keeps everyone happy: the church is happy because it thinks it's doing everyone a favour. Jeff is happy because I'm away from the hunks at the gym, and I'm happy because I'm away from Jeff and the kids and I don't have to pay membership at the Harbour Club to do it!

[she plays]

> What? To church? No way – only to see the twins in the nativity play. They were sheep – sooo sweet! No, this hall is the closest he's gonna get me to God … No, he never preaches at me. He knows I'm not interested.
>
> He just tells me how brilliant Jesus is and how much I'm missing out. And do you know – get this, Jude – on Monday nights I have to watch Eastenders in the bedroom 'cos of the Bible group

he has in the living room. Now that can't be right, can it? Still, all those church activities seem to keep him happy and he even takes the twins to Sunday school. On Sundays I pretty much get the house to myself, so Christianity does have its good points …

[she jumps as if to reach a very high shot]

Heck, that was a bit over-zealous! Don't worry, I'll get it.

[exit]

Mind the Gap

Nicki Matthews and Mandy Watsham

The action for this sketch takes place during the morning rush hour on the London Underground. All the characters will need to bump up and down as if on a Tube train.

It features four very different people who spend the journey observing the others and assessing what type of people they are, based on what they look like.

We, the audience, make similar assumptions about the characters and on what we expect them to be. As the journey comes to the end, however, we realise that you cannot judge people on appearance only, as each character turns out to be someone completely different from what we originally expected.

🧍‍♀️	🧍	⏱️
2	2*	4 minutes

* and a voice for the station announcer

Other themes

Appearances can be deceptive, relationships

Characters

JULIE:	Young woman in late twenties, director of her own successful company
MAUREEN:	Middle-aged nurse, tired and worn out
GEORGE:	Young fitness instructor, almost obsessed with the gym
HARRY:	Middle-aged alcoholic, used to be successful businessman but has lost job and family due to drink

Costumes

JULIE:	Smart trouser suit with coat over the top, handbag/briefcase
MAUREEN:	Nurse's uniform (or something similar) hidden by mac. Tights and sensible shoes
GEORGE:	Track pants and sweatshirt, trainers, cap, rucksack, head-phones
HARRY:	Long mac over suit. Brown battered shoes

All you need

❏ Two chairs
❏ Laptop computer (or bag to look like one)
❏ Walkman
❏ Hip flask

[Scene opens with JULIE and HARRY standing, holding on to imaginary overhead handles, jigging as if on a train. MAUREEN and GEORGE are sitting next to each other on a banquette.]

MAUREEN: *(looking at HARRY's feet)* Strange shoes! They don't go with that suit at all. Shame. He probably hasn't got a wife to help him with things like that. I expect he's an accountant – no, maybe a headmaster. That'll be it. Head of a private girls' school who lost his wife two years ago and needs a good woman to look after him. I bet he's got a nice house – probably lives somewhere out in the country. Burford *(or another 'well-heeled' country village familiar to your audience)* I'll be bound. I wonder what he's doing in London. Perhaps there's some sort of conference on. I bet he's a real gentleman – headmasters always are. *(she leans back and rests her eyes)*

JULIE: *(looking at GEORGE)* I don't like the look of him at all. Where's my bag? *(grabs her bag to her chest)* He looks like the type to grab it and run. I hate the Tube, you always get all sorts of unsavouries on it. The thing is, he's not that young – you'd think he'd know better. Mugging old ladies and smoking grass, and I bet he signs on. Good body, though – I suppose running from the police keeps him in good shape. Still, I think I'll get out at the next stop, just to be sure. I can always get a cab.

[MAUREEN has fallen asleep, leaning on GEORGE.]

GEORGE: Great, that's all I need – some silly bat falling asleep on me. I bet she snores, too! Grief, she's heavy! She needs to go on a good diet. She probably works in McDonald's, or maybe an old-fashioned country tea shop. No idea of how unhealthy cream cakes are for the heart! *(she flops)* She might have a bit more energy if she did something a bit more active. It's such a shame that women let themselves go when they get to a certain age. *(He gets up, taking off his headphones. JULIE flinches and clasps her bag even harder, but he gestures to her to have his seat; she sits down.)*

HARRY: Thanks very much – I would have liked to have sat down. Typical of the youth of today. Don't respect their elders. In my day, if you saw someone older and wiser than you, you gave up your seat for them. Still, things have changed, haven't they. Look at her, she can't be more than 25 and I bet she's got several kids. All from different fathers, no doubt! I expect she lives in a house subsidised by the council and still smokes 60 a day. She's probably on her way to Oxford Street to spend her Family Credit on a new pair of shoes for a night out with the girls. I don't know what the world's coming to.

MAUREEN: *(waking up with a start and looking around hoping no one has seen her)* Oh I'm stiff *(rubbing her neck)*. I really shouldn't have picked up Mrs Harris by myself. How many times have I told the junior nurses not to try and lift people on their own? I really should try and practise what I preach. Still – it's nice to sit down, even if it is in a crowded Tube train. I've been on my feet all night – I can't wait for a nice long bath and sleep. I hate the night shift.

JULIE: That was nice of him – perhaps I was wrong. He looks quite respectable without those headphones stuffed into his ears. I'm still holding on to my bag, though, just in case. If I lost my laptop I don't know what I'd do. My whole life is contained in there! Although I must admit it's terribly heavy to carry around the whole time – my shoulder really hurts. I should probably visit the physio at the gym later. I'm so glad I went ahead with the installation in the basement. One of my better decisions since taking over the company. That and the crèche. Old Mr Jones would never have agreed to it. He's probably turning in his grave! Engineers pumping iron before breakfast and reps visiting their babies during lunch hours! Most of the employees seem to appreciate it. A new ethos for the new millennium.

GEORGE: She looked ready for that sit-down. Tense or what! She needs a good work-out to get rid of some of that stress and tension. Perhaps I should give her my card. I've got a slot free on Tuesday lunchtimes, I think. If she works in the City I could probably fit her in for a personal fitness regime without too

much trouble. Or maybe she could just come along to the club —
she looks like she could afford the membership fees.

HARRY: Grief, I need get off this train! Is it me or is it getting hotter? I
really could do with a drink. What time is it? *(looking at watch)*
Great, now I'm going to be late. The agency won't like it. Oh,
who cares? I've managed without a job for the past year; I'm
sure I can carry on. If I can just get into my pocket … *(reaches
into his inside pocket for a hip flask which he pulls out)*

VOICE: This is Baker Street, Baker Street, change here for Circle, Central
and District lines. Baker Street.

[HARRY drinks from the flask and pushes past everyone to get off the train. Once off,
he stands drinking. The other three get off and pass him. He starts to reel backwards.
They turn round, and speak together with the voice.]

GEORGE, JULIE,
MAUREEN,
VOICE: Mind the gap!

[Blackout]

The Christmas Bash

Nicki Matthews

This sketch features Liz and Andrew, who are in the car on the way to the company Christmas bash. Andrew is obviously not keen on going, and we only find out the real reason for this right at the end of the sketch. It is not clear during the sketch whether it is Liz's or Andrew's company do; depending on the angle you are taking, there are three alternative endings to this sketch.

This sketch is a good example of a lack of communication between the two characters, as Liz valiantly tries to read the map while Andrew impatiently waits for instructions at the road junctions.

As Andrew clearly has an issue with the prospect of spending the evening with a group of people who drink too much, the sketch also highlights the challenges of 'fitting in' with a group of people who behave in a way you find inappropriate.

🧍‍♀️	🧍	🕐
1	1	3 minutes

Other themes

Christmas, relationships, drink

Characters

LIZ: In her thirties, Liz is quite a lively character. She is looking forward to the evening out

ANDREW: Similar age to Liz, but very on edge about the evening

Costumes

LIZ: Party dress, coat or cape over the top, hair-do for a night out

ANDREW: Dinner suit

All you need

❏ Two chairs next to each other to signify the front seats of a car
❏ Map/directions
❏ If possible: sound effect of Christmas carols playing from the car radio

[Scene opens with LIZ, pretending to look in visor mirror, adjusting hair, putting on lip-stick, etc. ANDREW is in place staring straight ahead and must mime driving a car, i.e. holding the steering wheel, looking in the mirror regularly, etc. Christmas carols are playing on the car radio.]

LIZ: *(glancing over)* Are you all right, love? You seem a bit on edge.

ANDREW: Yes, I'm fine – I just want to get this evening over with! Have you got the map there? I think we're coming into the town centre now so I'll need directions.

LIZ: Oh, now where did I put it? *(looking around her)*

ANDREW: I don't know. I gave it to you. I'm driving, you're navigating.

LIZ: OK, OK, don't get your knickers in a twist. I'll find it. *(bends down to look for it on the floor)*

ANDREW: I'm coming up to a roundabout – what exit shall I take?

LIZ: Hang on a minute … *(unhurriedly)*

ANDREW: *(getting frustrated)* I can't hang on a minute! I've got to go somewhere and I've got a big van right behind me.

LIZ: *(urgently shaking map out of its folds)* Oh, go round, I'll find it in a minute.

[ANDREW drives around the roundabout.]

ANDREW: Right – I'm coming back round to where we were. What now?

LIZ: Oh, sorry *(a bit panicky)* – I'm not sure – try left. No, hang on. Oh, go round again and I'll try and read the road signs. *(peering out)* Harefield Road – that's it! *(triumphantly)* Take that exit *(realising it's too late)* – the one we've just passed. Oh well, never mind, go round one more time and take the second exit, Harefield Road, OK? *(looking pleased with herself)*.

ANDREW: Right – now where?

LIZ: *(looking back down at the map)* Oh heck, let me just work it out. *(turning the map round to read it)* OK, carry on down this road and take the first turning on the *(pause. Points in front of her the* four points of the compass whilst muttering 'never eat shredded wheat', then gestures with right hand) right. I think it's quite soon.

ANDREW: *(looking out of the window)* Yes, it was quite soon – I've just passed the first turning on the right! *(through gritted teeth)*

LIZ: *(chirpily)* Well, you'll have to turn round, won't you.

ANDREW: Thank you for that. And here tonight, with the specialist subject of Stating the Absolutely Obvious – Liz Markham! *(turning car round)*

LIZ: What on earth is the matter with you? You've been in a foul mood all night. RED LIGHT! *(slams her foot down on imaginary brake pedal)*

ANDREW: *(sarcastic)* Thank you!

LIZ: Come on, what is it?

ANDREW: Nothing.

LIZ: Really? And what is it about this 'nothing' that makes you so bad-tempered?

ANDREW: Where now? I've come to a T-junction. I thought you were supposed to be navigating.

LIZ: And I thought I specialised in stating the absolutely obvious.

ANDREW: *(putting on a pathetic voice)* Please, honey bunch. Could you please look at the map and tell me where to go?

LIZ: With great pleasure! *(looking back at the map)* Um, left and then right at the traffic lights.

ANDREW: Thank you. *(indicates left and turns car)*

LIZ: So?

ANDREW: So what?

LIZ: So what's up?

ANDREW: I told you, I just want to get there, get it over with and get home!

LIZ: *(sarcastically)* Really looking forward to this evening, then!

ANDREW: How can you tell?

LIZ: Why, what's the problem?

ANDREW: The problem is the people and the politics. I can't bear all the interdepartmental bickering. It drives me mad.

LIZ: Andrew, it's a party, a Christmas party, for goodness sake! People will be there to have fun.

ANDREW: And that's another thing.

LIZ: What is?

ANDREW: These people come out with the express intention of getting completely smashed. They'll totally abuse the tab behind the bar, and at least half a dozen of them will end up throwing up in the toilets.

LIZ: Oh, come on, Andrew, I think you're exaggerating somewhat.

ANDREW: Really? Do I need to remind you of what happened last year? The whole hotel had to be evacuated when someone in a drunken stupor set off the fire alarm. I was surprised we weren't all thrown out! Where now?

LIZ: Straight over and it's just up here on the left. See, over there *(pointing)*.

ANDREW: Great, we're here already *(sarcastically)*.

LIZ: Look, if you hate it that much, why bother coming? You don't have to.

ANDREW: Yes I do.

LIZ: No, you don't. There's no law that states 'thou shalt attend the firm's annual Christmas bash'.

Ending 1
[They get out of the car and start to exit.]

ANDREW: Just the unwritten one.

LIZ: Which is?

ANDREW: I'm the boss!

Ending 2

ANDREW: I thought there was.

LIZ: No, really, Andrew. Don't trouble yourself. You go back home. There's no reason why you should endure this evening if you don't want to. It's my works do – I'll go on my own! Don't worry about me, I'll get a taxi back *(gets out of the car and exits)*. See you later.

[Blackout on Andrew]

Ending 3

ANDREW: Just the unwritten one ....

LIZ: Which is?

ANDREW: *(pulling on Santa hat and beard)* That I'm paid to play Father Christmas this year. Now come on, Trixabell, get your costume and follow me. *(LIZ glances at him as they both grab bags and walk off stage.)*

Hurry Sickness

Mandy Watsham and Nicki Matthews

The action for this sketch centres around a customer standing in the queue at the local supermarket.

There is a delay at the till, and as the queue gets longer the customer starts to display all the signs of having what is known in the twenty-first century as 'hurry sickness' – that is, having no patience at all. All the dialogue is as if the customer is thinking aloud, and so is not meant to be heard or acknowledged by any of the other characters.

The sketch simply illustrates that the society we live in seems to dictate that the speed we live at is getting faster and faster. Any small delays that ten or twenty years ago might have been small irritations now develop into major problems.

👩	👨	🕐
3*	2*	3 minutes

* or any combination of men and women

Other themes

Money, time management, snobbery

Characters

CASHIER:	Young YTS girl or boy with a not particularly high IQ
CUSTOMER 1:	Probably female. Quite timid and very embarrassed at holding up the queue
CUSTOMER 2:	Male or female, in a steaming hurry. Probably late for a meeting
MR JENKINS:	Elderly shop worker

Costumes

CASHIER:	Overall
CUSTOMER 1:	Casual clothes
CUSTOMER 2:	Smart suit
MR JENKINS:	Overall

All you need

❏ Table and chair to represent cash desk
❏ Till
❏ A supermarket basket
❏ Groceries, including a bag of sweets
❏ A newspaper

[The shop is not particularly busy. There is one person in the queue with a rather vague-looking checkout operator swiping groceries. He/she gets to the last item, which is a bag of sweets, and leafs through various lists to find the price code, but to no avail. CUSTOMER 2 joins the queue with a newspaper.]

CASHIER: Pick and mix, um … no idea … what price code … um …

CUSTOMER 1:   *(smiles)*

CUSTOMER 2:   *(sighs loudly)*

CASHIER: *(speaking into intercom)* Mr Jenkins to checkout 1, please. Mr Jenkins to checkout 1. *(smiles apologetically at CUSTOMER 1 and avoids eye contact with CUSTOMER 2, who makes a point of looking at watch; CASHIER desperately scans store for any sign of MR JENKINS)*

CUSTOMER 2:   (thinking aloud) Oh, for goodness sake, how much longer do we have to wait? I knew I should have gone next door to Woolworths for this paper. *(pauses, looking at the bag of pick and mix sweets)* That's where she should have gone for her pick and mix – they do a much better selection in there. *(pauses, still waiting for price check)* Why would you ever want to get pick and mix from this supermarket? Are you not aware that you're not only missing out on coconut mushrooms but also pink shrimps from this particular variety of pick and mix?

CUSTOMER 1:   *(smiles apologetically at CUSTOMER 2)*

CUSTOMER 2:   *(smiles back)* The only coconut you'll get in that pick and mix is the loose fibres from the coconut matting in the doorway.

CASHIER: *(continues scanning the store with even more earnest neck-craning)*

CUSTOMER 1:   *(looks slightly sheepish)*

CASHIER: *(trying the intercom again)* Mr Jenkins, please come to checkout 1 – urgent price enquiry.

CUSTOMER 2:   All for a bag of pick and mix. Do me and your thighs a favour, my dear, and leave the sweets behind.

CASHIER: *(trying the intercom again and now with desperation in voice)* Mr Jenkins, please come to checkout 1 – urgent price enquiry, please.

CUSTOMER 2: Oh, come on, this is getting ridiculous – five minutes, all for a newspaper. I'd be better off getting it delivered at this rate. Blow the extra ninepence, it'd be worth it! *(pause)* This is a complete waste of my time. *(muttering)* Come on, come on, come on *(gradually getting up to shouting pitch)* COME ON, MR JENKINS, WHERE ON EARTH ARE …

[MR JENKINS ambles slowly to the cash desk.]

CUSTOMER 2: *(sarcastically)* Oh, that's right, you take your time. After all, I've really got nothing better to do than stand in this queue. In fact, I would go as far to say that I have really learned to love it here.

[MR JENKINS runs his finger down the list but can't seem to find the right code.]

MR JENKINS: Pick and mix, eh … no idea. *(into intercom)* Miss Brown, please contact checkout 1, Miss Brown to checkout 1. I'll open up checkout 2. If you've less than five items in your basket, then, um, if you'd like to come over –

[CUSTOMER 2 goes to move but is obviously beaten by someone with a full basket.]

CUSTOMER 2: Well, if that just isn't the brassiest neck! She could see I've only got a paper, and I'm sure she's got *(craning neck as if to count items)* more than five items in her basket. *(turning to imaginary customer standing behind in the queue)* Lend me your cucumber, madam, I have some serious business to attend to!

[Meanwhile the CASHIER is starting to panic and tries again to find the price code. Suddenly she spots it.]

CASHIER: I've got it, I've got it!

CUSTOMER 2: I don't doubt it, dear – just don't come near me!

CASHIER: I've found the code. *(as if in explanation)* I've not done pick and mix before – I've only just been promoted to tills. It's a bit of a responsibility.

CUSTOMER 2: Where do they get their staff! I'm all for equal opportunities, but this is ridiculous.

[CASHIER puts the amount into the till and totals the bill.]

CASHIER: That's £17.61 altogether, please.

CUSTOMER 1: £17.61 – Oh dear, I …

CUSTOMER 2: Oh no.

CUSTOMER 1: … think …

CUSTOMER 2: Please!

CUSTOMER 1: … I may …

CUSTOMER 2: Not that!

CUSTOMER 1: … have to …

CUSTOMER 2: I can't take this!

CUSTOMER 1: … put something back.

CUSTOMER 2: No!

CASHIER: Oh.

CUSTOMER 1: A few of the pick and mix, perhaps.

CUSTOMER 2: AAARRRGGGHHH!

[Blackout]

CHAPTER 12

a matter of life and death

For slightly more serious subjects, this section contains three songs and three sketches based on themes of life and death and who we really are.

As we move further into the new millennium, many people are asking the questions 'What's life all about?' and 'Where am I going?' These songs and sketches can be used particularly well in seeker services to illustrate some of these feelings and show where God fits in.

SONGS

❏   Great is Thy Faithfulness
❏   May the Mind of Christ My Saviour
❏   Beyond the Grip of Grace

SCRIPTS

Hatched, Matched, Dispatched
Whether you are a regular churchgoer or not, some of the most significant of our memories feature the church. This is a comical vicar
remembering the three appearances of a member of his congregation
when she was hatched, matched and finally dispatched.

In the Year 3000ce
A look at the possible outcome of 'the end of the world' and how the few
remaining survivors are coping 500 years later.

It's My Life
A mother trying to live her life again through her daughter, who is
therefore not free to be herself as her mother attempts to push her into
a mould.

Great Is Thy Faithfulness

Words by Thomas O. Chisholm, music by Mandy Watsham

This is a reworking of the wonderful old hymn, using the same words but dramatically changing the music to turn it into a haunting, powerful ballad.

We have used this song many times, and always someone will comment on how it has made the hairs on the back of their neck stand on end. It is wonderfully effective when used following 'Christmas in Captivity', a monologue based on Terry Waite's experiences and also included in this book, as the two together highlight the fact that, even when everything else is taken away from you, God's faithfulness remains unchanging and everlasting.

The introduction works particularly well when played on a sax, oboe or other woodwind instrument, but a pan flute or some similar voice on the keyboard can be just as effective.

Verse 1 and the chorus are sung as a solo, very simply, to just a piano accompaniment. This song really builds, so when we perform it we add drums with verse 2 to establish a more contemporary beat. Verse 2 is also sung as a solo, and the second chorus is sung as a duet with a top harmony line.

Verse 3 is 'all guns blazing', with three or more voices singing harmonies and a full band building up to a powerful third chorus. After the last chorus the song finishes, taking the coda as it began, simply, with just the piano accompanying, and one lone voice singing plaintively, 'Great is thy faithfulness, Lord, unto me, Lord, unto me.'

Great Is Thy Faithfulness

great   is   thy   faith - ful - ness;

morn - ing__ by   morn - ing__ new   mer - cies__ I__ see.

All   I__ have need - ed   thy   hand hast pro - vi - ded;

3rd time **to Coda** ⊕

great   is__ thy   faith - ful - ness,   Lord,__ un - to   me.

⊕ **CODA**   *rit.*

me.   Great   is__ thy   faith - ful - ness,   Lord,__ un - to

me,_____   Lord,__ un - to   me.

Verse 1
Great is thy faithfulness, O God my Father,
there is no shadow of turning with thee.
Thou changest not, thy compassions they fail not;
as thou has been thou forever wilt be.

Chorus
Great is thy faithfulness,
great is thy faithfulness;
morning by morning new mercies I see.
All I have needed thy hand hast provided;
great is thy faithfulness, Lord, unto me.

Verse 2
Summer and winter and spring time and harvest,
sun, moon and stars in their courses above
join with all nature in manifold witness
to thy great faithfulness, mercy and love.

Chorus

Verse 3
Pardon for sin and a peace that endureth,
thine own dear presence to cheer and to guide,
strength for today and bright hope for tomorrow:
blessings all mine, with ten thousand beside.

Chorus

Coda
Great is thy faithfulness, Lord, unto me,
Lord, unto me.

May the Mind of Christ My Saviour

Words by Kate B. Wilkinson, music by Mandy Watsham

A new version of an old hymn, in the style of a bright ballad using fantastic words that challenge all of us to live with 'The mind of Christ my Saviour'.

You may notice that verses 2 and 3 have been reversed in order in this version. This is because verse 2 works better, words wise, in the more upbeat, stronger and louder bridge section: 'May the word of God dwell richly in my heart from hour to hour, so that all may see I triumph only through his power.'

The song finishes on a key change, which emphasises the hope we have as we run the race before us, looking only unto Jesus.

This song is really more of a challenge to people who are involved in outreach or mission rather than a song to be included in a Chrysalis event. However, if you are looking for a challenge in the seeker service, perhaps, then this song could be appropriate.

May the Mind of Christ My Saviour

VERSE

1. May the mind of Christ my_ Sav-iour live in me from day to day,
2. May the peace of God . . .
3. May the love of Je - sus . . .

by His love and_ power con - trol - ling all I do or say.

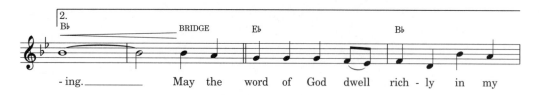

- ing._____ May the word of God dwell rich - ly in my

heart from hour to__ hour, so that all may see__ I tri - umph,

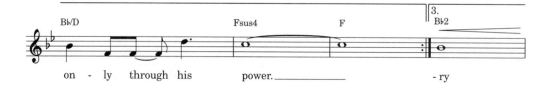

on - ly through his power._____ - ry

4. May I run the race be-fore me, strong and brave to

face the foe, look-ing on-ly__ un-to Je-sus as I on-ward

go.____ May I run the race be-fore me,

strong and brave to face the foe, look-ing on-ly__

un-to Je-sus as I on-ward go,____

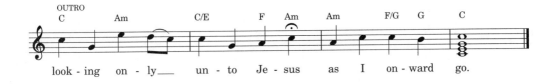

look-ing on-ly__ un-to Je-sus as I on-ward go.

Verse 1
May the mind of Christ my Saviour
live in me from day to day,
by His love and power controlling
all I do or say.

Verse 2
May the peace of God my Father
rule my life in everything,
that I may be calm to comfort
sick and sorrowing.

Bridge
May the word of God dwell richly
in my heart from hour to hour,
so that all may see I triumph,
only through his power.

Verse 3
May the love of Jesus fill me
as the waters fill the sea,
him exalting, self abasing,
this is victory

Verse 4
May I run the race before me,
strong and brave to face the foe,
looking only unto Jesus
as I onward go.

Repeat verse 4

... looking only into Jesus
as I onwards go.

Beyond the Grip of Grace

Words and music by Mandy Watsham

This song is a gospel-style ballad. After the first four bars of the introduction, bring in three-part harmony to complete the introduction with four bars of gospel-style 'oohs'.

This song is ideally suited to a duet because of the range involved.

The theme is faith without seeing, security in God's love, knowing that no matter who we are or what we've done, we can never fall beyond the 'grip of his grace'.

Verse 1 commences with Voice 1, and Voice 2 joins in for the chorus. The song builds through verse 2 and chorus 2, and the bridge is powerful and punchy, sung in three-part harmony, as written.

The piece rejoices in the security of God's overwhelming love for us, safe and secure in his 'grip of grace', and in wonderment at the creation that surrounds us and the knowledge that the hand that cared enough to create the stars also cared enough to create us. He is waiting, ever ready, to listen for our call.

The chorus ends the song, with the final line of the chorus repeated at the slower speed to reiterate the message of the song: 'knowing in this embrace I never will fall beyond the grip of grace'.

Beyond the Grip of Grace

♩. = 60

1. Some-where, out in the si - lence,_ out in the dark-ness,_ be-yond the
2. Arms . . .

stars,_____ some - where,_ a love lies_ wait-ing,_ rea-dy for

Verse 1
Somewhere, out in the silence,
out in the darkness, beyond the stars,
somewhere, a love lies waiting,
ready for anything, listening for my call.

Chorus
And when it seems life is unkind,
future's unsure, people rewind,
need something sure, a love that's secure,
that won't let me down.
That's when I reach beyond the stars
to find a love beyond my heart,
knowing in this embrace I never will fall
beyond the grip of grace.

Verse 2
Arms of love, protecting my frailty,
restoring my dignity, renewing a strength in me.
O in this embrace, where purity means poverty,
this love brings out the best in me.
How could I live without?

Chorus

Bridge
How do you explain the mystery of this love,
so misunderstood by millions through all time?
Can we truly represent the sacrifice?
Can we really show love's magnitude
that means we're safe at last,
at last?

Chorus
Knowing in this embrace I never will fall
beyond the grip of grace.

Hatched, Matched and Dispatched

David Robinson

Whether we are regular churchgoers or not, some of the most significant of our memories feature the church in some way, be it christenings, weddings or funerals.

This monologue features a comical vicar remembering the only three appearances of a member of his congregation – when she was hatched, matched and finally dispatched.

Although this sketch is comical, it ends on a poignant note as Eve – the central character – has obviously met an untimely end.

This is really a challenge to those who attend church on high days and holidays but see no place for it on a regular basis.

👤	👤	⏱
0	1	4 minutes

Other themes

Christening, marriage, church attendance, death

Characters

REV. SPORE: elderly vicar, rather forgetful but very warm-hearted

Costumes

Ideally, black cassock and dog collar

All you need

❏ Scrap of paper

[REV. SPORE is standing holding an imaginary baby in his arms.]

REV. SPORE: Well, my dear friends, parents, godparents, grandparents, great-grandparents, ever so great- grandparents, welcome to this joyous occasion: the christening of this beautiful if somewhat original-looking little baby.

[He is looking at the baby and is obviously told by someone in the congregation that he has the baby upside down and is not looking at the face, but at the other end. He carefully turns the baby around.]

I do beg your pardon. Well, in the presence of this congregation I take great pleasure in baptising this child … *(he fishes in his pocket for his note and reads from a screwed up piece of paper)* Maxwell. I baptise this child Maxwell House, two pounds of sugar and … oh, I do beg your pardon. I baptise this child Eva. May God bless Eva and her proud parents, Mr and Mrs Stick. *(slowing realising what her name will sound like)* How lovely. May God bless Eva Stick and give her a wonderful sense of humour when she gets older. My, how she'll need it.

[Lights fade momentarily. REV. SPORE spins around to illustrate the passing of time.]

Remember Eva? Eva got married today. She came down the aisle with a big broad smile, went out through the big west door. She got married today. She changed her name to Eve some years ago. She got married today to that nice young man Steve Hoe. Now she's Eve Hoe. She got married today, came down the aisle with a big broad smile, went out through the big west door. I read their banns once, twice and thrice. They never came near, just rang and asked about throwing rice. She got married today came down the aisle with a big broad smile, went out through the big west door. Said, 'Vicar, we'll be back for more,' Steve and Eve Hoe, but I don't know. I saw her hatched, now I've seen her matched, went out through the big west door. I think I'll see her once more.

[Lights fade momentarily. REV. SPORE spins around to illustrate the passing of time.]

Eva, Eva, always eager. Now she's gone, no chance to retrieve her. Eva. Was here such a short while, no longer than that big broad smile. I saw her as a babe in arms, held her for a while; saw her coming down the aisle, big broad smile. Out through the big west door. Eva, Eva, always eager. Now she's gone, no chance to retrieve her. Eva. Was here such a short while, no longer than that big broad smile. I saw her hatched, I saw her matched, and now, Eva, Eva, dispatched.

[Fade out]

In the Year 3000CE

Judith Watsham, Mandy Watsham and Nicki Matthews

This sketch is quite different from the others in this book, and as such would be more suited to a seeker service than a cabaret. Tackling a much more serious subject, it takes a look at the possible outcome of 'the end of the world'.

Based in the year 3000, the action takes place on a hilltop, five hundred years after what many people would call 'Armageddon'. Only a few hundred people have survived, and the sketch shows how these few remaining survivors are coping.

The sketch is based on the assumption that the Christian gospel was buried, along with churches and scriptures, when the end came. Indeed, the survivors assume that if there is a 'God' or some kind of powerful being in existence, then he must be a terrifying force to be reckoned with. After all, he ended the world and left them to live their pitiful existence on their own, didn't he?

However, as the action unfolds, we watch four young people as they discover a 'millennium pod' – the kind that was buried by many children and adults at the end of 1999 – containing, among other things, copies of the four Gospels. As they read the totally unfamiliar words for the very first time, they start to believe that perhaps there is something more to offer them hope.

⛄	⛄	🕐
2*	2*	5 minutes

* or any combination of 4 people + voice

Characters

All four main characters can be male or female, and ideally all are in their late teens/early twenties.

LUCE:	A leader, taller and stronger than the others
MARCH:	A thinker
MATHER:	A follower
JONA:	A sceptic
VOICE:	Should either be heard and not seen or, if this is not possible, should stand or sit well out of the way of the stage action. The audience's attention should be focused on the four main actors

Costumes

All four should be dressed in a similar fashion in tunics and sandals. The tunics can be made of what should appear to be non biodegradable plastic bags or 'ethnic' rugs. Rough belts around their waists hold very basic digging tools.

All you need

❑ A pile of 'rocks' made from boxes to represent a hillside or hilltop, some of which should be removed in the search (optional – this could be mimed)

❑ A 'millennium pod' which should be large enough to contain the remaining items

❑ Four Gospels, each wrapped in a plastic bag, the whole in another bag (should be the last item out)

❑ Several twentieth-century items which could have survived in the pod; the selection of these can be the choice of the cast but thought should be given to what could survive for five hundred years. They could, but do not have to, include: a Bic pen, a travel hairdryer or iron with plug attached, a computer disk, a video tape, a CD, a Walkman, a camera (perhaps a disposable one), a chain of paperclips, a 'snowstorm' paperweight and a mobile phone

❏ A tattered piece of paper or sheet of plastic which has details of the pod's contents, etc. (should be the first item to be removed)

[The scene opens with the four characters standing motionless in a line behind a pile of 'rocks'. The stage area is blacked out, or very dim.]

VOICE: Imagine. Three thousand years ago a baby was born somewhere on the Earth. This child was important for well over two thousand years, but now he is only a folk memory, associated with a red costume and a children's festival. No one living has ever seen a land mass in the area where tradition places him; only a few rocky islands remain since the world was flooded five hundred years ago when disaster struck the Earth. A meteor, hurled from beyond the stars, caused the seas to rise and the lands, except for the highest mountainous regions, to be covered by the sea as the ice caps melted and the temperatures rose. Earth's teeming billions were reduced to a few hundred scattered survivors, all of whom firmly believe in a terrifying, vengeful, destructive force which must constantly be placated in order to avoid repetition of the disaster. In other words, the world's survivors have reverted to paganism.

[The stage becomes brighter as the characters move from behind the rocks in single file. They are slightly out of breath, as if they have climbed a hill. LUCE is in the lead, followed closely by MARCH and MATHER, the latter looking nervously around. JONA brings up the rear and is obviously convinced they are wasting their time. All of them are serious-faced and unhappy.]

LUCE: I don't care what you say – my father always said, and he said his father told him, that there was something buried on the top of this mountain, something that would help future generations when they really needed it.

JONA: Well, if they were that sure there's something up here, why didn't they look for it, then? I really don't believe there IS anything here at all. We're wasting our time. Why don't we head back?

MATHER: It's pretty easy to work out why they didn't come up here to look for it themselves. They were scared rigid! Their parents told them not to do anything to make ... you know ... *(looks around uneasily and drops voice to a stage whisper and coughs as if masking a name)* … notice them. It must have been the same since … Well … It's only now, since we heard that the southerners didn't have to do anything at all to make the sun and the rain come back because it happened whatever they did or didn't do … It's only now that we know that there isn't any … *(looks around uneasily again, drops voice, coughs, as before)* … anything to worry about.

JONA: *(scoffing)* Oh yeah? Well then, why are you whispering?

[MATHER and JONA square up for a fight but are separated when LUCE steps between them and forces them apart.]

LUCE: Oh, do stop it. You know we agreed we'd look, and if there is … *(glances around)* … anyone, thing, whatever, then we agreed that we didn't care. Life's hopeless and pointless enough, anyway.

[during the above MARCH has been poking around, moving rocks and stones]

MARCH: I think there is something here, you know. Your old man was right.

[The others forget their quarrel and go and help move more rocks out of the way. MARCH triumphantly pulls a 'pod' out of the ground.]

MARCH: Get a load of this!

(He opens it with difficulty and pulls out a tattered piece of paper. JONA grabs it, turns it round, squints at it despairingly.)

MARCH: *(angrily)* Oi!

JONA: I can't make sense of this.

[MARCH takes it back and studies it.]

MARCH: I think I can … *(reads slowly)* this pod was filled up and buried by the chi … chil … something … of – oh no, I don't believe this!

It looks like *(name of a local town).*

LUCE: It can't be! That's what my old man's place is called.

JONA: Your old man's place should be called 'pigsty', if you ask me!

MARCH: We didn't! But it would make sense if it had something to do with that area. It's his family who've always said that there was something here, anyway. *(looks at the paper again)* Oh! This was buried by, must be 'children', of *(name of local town)* in the ... *(hesitantly)* year? Oh yes, that's right, I know that people used to divide time into odd periods called years and months – don't know why – of Our Lord ... *(aside)* ... what's an our lord? ... 2000? *(voice ends on a question mark)*

MATHER: My father says that we used to number the years, adding another number every twelve months.

LUCE: Our ancestors were really weird!

JONA: *(no longer mocking and scoffing but interested)* Never mind all that. Is there anything else in there?

[They sit down in order to pull out various items. The characters are obviously puzzled by the uses of most of them. After they have put aside everything else there is one large plastic-wrapped package left. MARCH unwraps it.]

MARCH: What's this? Books? *(pulls out four separate Gospels, each wrapped in a plastic bag which he removes, placing the books on the floor as he does so)* You know, we should take these to my father, he's in charge of all the books we have.

[LUCE reaches over and picks up one of the books and starts looking at it.]

MATHER: My father says that he believes that once there were thousands of books in the world.

JONA: Oh, yeah? He really comes out with some choice statements, your father!

[they look as if they will fight again]

LUCE: *(looks up impatiently)* Don't start all that again, for goodness
sake! Let me read what's in it. Hey, this book is called Luke –
that's a bit like my name. Listen to this. It's a bit like that old
story – you know, the one about the baby – but there's no red
cloak or feasts here. It says …

JONA: *(interrupting)* WHAT, that old children's tale? My mother used to
tell me that story sometimes, when I was little.

LUCE: It's not quite the same. Just listen, will you? It says that after the
baby was born some shepherds who were spending the night in
the fields saw an angel, who told them not to be afraid because
he had good news for all people. 'This very day in David's town
a Saviour was born – Christ the Lord! And this is what will prove
it to you: you will find a baby wrapped in strips of cloth and
lying in a manger.' Then the shepherds go to see for themselves
and they hear more angels singing about peace on earth – that's
more than we were told when we were kids, isn't it? *(flicks more
pages)* Look here, and here, when this baby grew up he travelled
around healing people and talking to them about love, then –
oh no – he was killed!

JONA: *(mockingly)* So what? We've all got to die sometime!

[While LUCE and JONA are talking, MARCH has picked up another book and looked at the
first page; he then quickly picks up the next book, and again looks at the first page.
JONA quietly gets hold of the fourth book and copies MARCH; he is grinning, and gives
the impression that he wants to prove that it is a big fairy story, but as he reads on
he gets more involved.]

LUCE: Oh no, it's all right. Listen – after he had been killed some
women went to, um – oh, it must be the place where he was
buried – but the body had gone; they met two men in shining
clothes who told them, 'Remember what he said to you … the
Son of Man must be handed over to sinners, be crucified, and
three days later rise to life.' He was dead and then he was alive
again!

MARCH: If you think that's unlikely, what about this? It's really weird.
Your name is Luce, your book is called Luke; I'm March, this

book is called Mark; *(pointing)* your name is Mather, this book is Matthew *(passes the book over)*, and *(looks around for the fourth book)* – oh, I see! What have you got, Jona?

JONA: *(in a strange, slightly scared voice)* This one is John.

[pause while they all look at each other and then turn back to looking through the books]

[Lights should dim if possible and come up to denote the passing of time. All four have obviously read a long way through their books.]

JONA: *(to MARCH)* Your father keeps all our books and told us stories when we were kids. How come he didn't tell us this one?

MARCH: I suppose he didn't know it.

MATHER: But this story must have been written nearly three thousand years ago, and those children who buried this little lot must have known it and …

JONA: *(still interrupting, but no longer mocking and sceptical)* They must have known it was important. Some of our ancestors probably did read these books, but if they did, they didn't pass on any mention of them.

LUCE: Well, now we have found them we can't forget about it. I'm sure I read somewhere in here *(waves his book)* that once you've read this, you shouldn't keep it to yourself …

MARCH: I don't feel like I want to keep it to myself. You know … I just feel … something … I'm not sure what. *(the others all nod and ad lib 'Yes', 'So do I', etc.)* I've never understood why, but sometimes the stories in my father's books make me feel strange, and this makes me feel a bit like that: happy, I think, and something else – oh, I can't explain it, but …

MATHER: *(quietly, almost dreamily)* I feel like I'm looking forward to something, but I don't know what it is, like something good is just around the corner, hoping, maybe. l feel hopeful. It says here *(opens book)* 'that he came so that we could have life and have it abundantly'. I can't imagine what it would be like to have abundant life – but I wouldn't mind trying it!

JONA: Yeah! It says here that he brought light into the world and can give eternal life to those who believe in him. Life with a purpose, that's what I want, not just an existence with no idea where I'm going or what anything is for.

[They all ad lib again: 'Me too!', 'Yes, you're right', 'Come on, then!' They scramble up, laughing, obviously feeling happy and excited, picking up the pod and other contents.]

LUCE: Come on, we've been up here for hours. If we don't get a move on they'll be sending out a search party.

[Exit, ad libbing: 'It says here ...' etc. Blackout.]

VOICE: Imagine. An intelligent yet pagan people, hearing the story of Jesus for the first time ...

[End]

It's My Life!

Mandy Watsham and Nicki Matthews

This is a duologue featuring a middle-aged mother and her teenage daughter. Both are on the telephone to their respective friends, each talking about the other.

As she chats to her WI colleague, it becomes obvious that Jill, the mother, is trying to make her daughter into something she's not. She believes her to be 'just like I was' – interested in making jam and arranging flowers.

Charley, on the other hand, couldn't be more different from her mother. She enjoys going to clubs and has a boyfriend she knows her mother wouldn't approve of.

It seems that Jill is trying to live her life again through her daughter and is attempting to push her into a mould. Charley is not free to be herself and develop her own personality.

The sketch can be used as an ideal introduction to a talk highlighting how God designed us to be individuals, and how we can only be truly free to be ourselves in Christ.

🧍‍♀️	🧍	🕐
2	0	4 minutes

Other themes

Families, individuality

Characters

| JILL: | Middle-aged mother who thinks she knows best for her teenage daughter |
| CHARLEY: | 'Normal' 18-year-old girl soon to leave for university, torn between being herself and not upsetting her mum |

Costumes

| JILL: | Country attire: tweed skirt, jumper, sensible shoes |
| CHARLEY: | Whatever the current trend is – not what Mother would approve of! Include a pair of Doc Marten boots (DMs) if possible |

All you need

❏ Two telephones
❏ Pieces of wood

[Lights up on JILL, who is on the telephone.]

JILL: Hello, Doreen, Jill here. How are you, dear? Good. Oh, can't complain. My hip's giving me gyp, but I know that's because I've been overdoing it with my Jane Fonda video. Listen, just wondering how all the arrangements are going for the WI flower and garden produce show next week. They are? Oh good, good. That's absolutely fine. Listen, I was just wondering if you could do with any extra help at all, because my Charlotte is very keen to be involved. You know, arranging the jams and making the teas, that sort of thing. You could? Oh super, that's lovely. I know she'll be thrilled. Loves doing her bit for the community. Yes. Even as we speak she's sorting out all the gadget wood for next week's Girl Guide camp. You know, welly-boot racks, draining boards, that sort of thing. I used to love Guide camp with a passion. Highlight of my hols, it was. I remember the time I was sharing a tent with Big Brenda – human larder, she was, could eat a whole swiss roll at once by cramming it lengthways into her mouth! Those were the days. Childhood innocence, happy memories …

[Lights fade down on her and up on to CHARLEY, who is also on the phone talking to a friend. She is dressed in DMs and is absentmindedly twirling gadget wood in her hand.]

CHARLEY: Hi, Rach, Charley here. Going down the club tonight? Too right I'll be there. Can't wait another week before I see Rob, and it's the only chance I'm going to get to see him. Mother seems to deny his whole existence. Just because he's got a motorbike and goes to art college, he doesn't seem to meet her criteria. She still thinks I'm going out with Martin. I'm sure she only likes him 'cos he works in a bank! Like that's a measure of respectability – if only she knew! What, now? Oh nothing much, just sorting out the *(mutters)* the gadget wood for next week's Guide camp. *(embarrassed)* Oh you know, boot and bedding racks, that sort of thing. Yeah, I know you wouldn't do it but … well, my mum … it seems to mean a lot to her, so the way I see it, I lose a few hours and she keeps off my back. That way, everyone's happy. As long as she doesn't get me involved in the WI – that is one thing I would draw the line at! Give me gadget wood and Guide camp over garden produce and greengage jam any day! The only arrangements I want to be making with jam is smearing it all over Rob's torso ... have you seen his six-pack...?

[lights fade down on her and back up on JILL]

JILL: Yes, of course she'll have time. What nightclub? The Purple Palace – that dreadful cellar place under the curtain shop in the high street? She'd never go there. Are you sure? Well, I expect she went just the once to keep her friends company. It's not her sort of thing at all: she much prefers gardening and shopping with me. A proper little housewife, that's my Charlotte. Yes, I am sure. Look, Doreen, I'm not sure what you're driving at but I think I know my daughter a little better than you! Yes, I appreciate you're only trying to help but you're implying that I don't know what's best for her. She's just like I was at 18. Whoever gets my girl as a wife will be getting a very good deal with the life training I'm giving her. I remember my mother saying to me, 'Jill, a girl can never have too many pairs of Marigolds ...'

CHARLEY: Anyway, you're OK for me to tell Mum I'm staying at yours tonight, aren't you? It would really burst her bubble if she found out I was staying at Rob's. I know I've been seeing him for six months but I still don't think the time's right. Because, well, she'd be so disappointed in me. She's got this idea about how my life should be going, which involves gadget wood, gardening and Girl Guides, and I just can't be like that. Because she just wouldn't understand. I just know she wouldn't. She doesn't realise that I'm different from her. *(grunts)* She thinks I'm just like her when she was my age.

JILL: No, of course I've never asked her. I don't need to. I know what she likes.

CHARLEY: The thing is, she doesn't understand me. She never asks how I feel and what I think about things. Just assumes she knows.

JILL: Of course I haven't driven her away. She's going to university because she wants to study sociology, and I know she'll come home every weekend.

CHARLEY: I can't wait till university next month. Then I can do what I like, I can be free – well, you know – free *(pause)* free to be me.

JILL: Well, we'll see. She's my little girl and I only want what's best for her.

CHARLEY: Well, maybe I'll talk to her in a few months, when I've been away for a while. I don't want to upset her.

JILL: NO, REALLY, I KNOW WHAT I'M DOING.

[Blackout]

CHAPTER 13

high days and holidays

This section is for cabarets or services being held on special days. These four songs and six sketches cover such events as Christmas, Easter and Remembrance Sunday.

All too often, it's difficult to find something different to perform at times ike Easter and Christmas. We hope these new songs and sketches will give you something to get your teeth into.

SONGS

- ❏ Remember Me
- ❏ I Wonder as I Wander
- ❏ The Nativity Play
- ❏ We Will Remember Them

SCRIPTS

The Christmas Ox
A Christmas Grotto ox is played by a young person just out of drama school, trying to attract the attention of the passing shoppers but obviously totally disillusioned with the whole thing.

'Er Indoors
First-hand observations of the events on the first Good Friday from the wife of the person who put Jesus to death

Christmas in Captivity
A monologue adapted from Terry Waite's account of his third Christmas in captivity in Beirut.

Star of the Show
Two five-year-olds discussing who is the most important character in the school nativity play.

Remembrance Day?
Four people's memories of different wars and how they have had a long-lasting effect of their lives and the lives of those close to them. The action takes place during the two-minute silence.

The Night before Christmas
Loosely based on the BBC TV sitcom *The Royle Family*, the Crownes are a typical family celebrating Christmas. We see bickering between siblings, strained relationships and an aversion to attending church if it disturbs the Christmas TV.

Remember Me

Words by John Newton, music by Mandy Watsham

This is a little-known poem by one of the great hymn-writers, John Newton. The original music, if indeed there ever was any, has long since been mislaid, and I came across the words through a John Newton scholar who was looking for the poem to be set to new music. So I duly obliged, as the words seemed to clearly dictate an appropriate tune and accompaniment.

The song is bright, bubbly and cheery, and the quavers glide smoothly through the introduction and along into the song itself.

The words clearly tell the story of the thief who was hanging on a cross beside Jesus. As he dies, he asks Jesus to 'Remember me.' Jesus replies, 'I tell you the truth, today you will be with me in paradise.' The song goes on to say 'my sins are not less black than those which brought him' – the thief – 'to the tree'. But we can still say the same words to Jesus as the thief did: 'O Lord, remember me.'

Theme-wise, it gives a fairly direct gospel message focusing on forgiveness, and is, not surprisingly, very appropriate for Easter. It offers hope for eternal life and peace. No matter how good we think we are compared to the condemned criminal, the fact is that we *all* fall short of Jesus' perfect example and must all ask for his forgiveness. By God's grace, we all receive it.

The final verse sings joyfully of a Saviour who will 'remember me' when we meet him face to face in eternity.

Permission to transcribe 'The thief who near the Saviour hung' by John Newton, MS. Eng. poet. c. 51 pp. 253–6 in a musical setting has been kindly granted by the Bodleian Library, University of Oxford.

Remember Me

Bright and cheery! ♩ = 130

thief____ who__ near the Sav - iour hung (in
(2.) Je - sus__ died, . . .
(3.) Lamb____ up - on . . .

death, how_ ha - ppy_ he!)_____ was ans - wered

when his dy - ing tongue said, 'Lord,____ re - mem - ber

me.'_____ My sins are not___ less black than

Verse 1
The thief who near the Saviour hung
(in death, how happy he!)
was answered when his dying tongue
said, 'Lord, remember me.'
My sins are not less black than those
which brought him to the tree,
no thought can give my heart repose
but, Lord, remember me.

Verse 2
When Jesus died, death lost its sting
like the enraged bee,
and I may now address the King
with, 'Lord, remember me.'
I take my pattern from the thief –
I have no other plea –
for I of sinners am the chief;
then, Lord, remember me.

Verse 3
The Lamb upon his glorious throne
as newly slain I see,
and trust he will not those disown
who plead 'Remember me.'
And when before him face to face
I bow my thankful knee,
in joyful strains I'll praise his grace
Who now remembers me.

I Wonder as I Wander

Words from traditional Appalachian carol, music by Mandy Watsham

This is a new version of the traditional Christmas carol, retaining the original words but using a more modern, folky new tune.

The piece is written in 6/8 time, which gives a nice bright feeling to the song. The semi-quavers written for the intro and outro of the song should be maintained into the first part of all the verses to ensure that the song moves along brightly.

The piece switches between major and minor keys to highlight certain phrases in the song: e.g. 'If Jesus had wanted for any wee thing' is written in the minor key, changing into the major key for 'or all of God's angels in heaven to sing' to create a bright hopeful sound, and so on.

The majority of the piece can be sung as a solo, but it would be enhanced if another voice or two was added to the bridge part referred to above. When we have performed this song, a second and third voice echoes 'any wee thing' and 'bird on the wing', and then we sing 'or all of God's angels in heaven to sing' choral-style, with as many voices as possible, going back to one voice for 'he surely could have it ...' The last verse following the choral piece could do with some backing vocal 'oohs' behind it, to support the soloist.

The song ends as it started, with the bright brisk semi-quavers playing out.

I Wonder as I Wander

Verse 1
I wonder as I wander out under the sky
how Jesus the Saviour did come for to die,
for poor orn'ery people like you and like I;
I wonder as I wander out under the sky.

Verse 2
When Mary birthed Jesus 'twas in a cow's stall
with wise men and cattle and shepherds and all,
but high from God's heaven a star's light did fall
and the promise of ages it then did recall.

Verse 3
If Jesus had wanted for any wee thing,
a star in the sky or a bird on the wing,
for all of God's angels in heaven did sing,
he surely could have it for he was the King.

Verse 4
I wonder as I wander out under the sky
how Jesus the Saviour did come for to die
for poor orn'ery people like you and like I;
I wonder as I wander out under the sky.

The Nativity Play

Words and music by Peter Laws

This song is a light, contemporary song with a shuffle beat behind it, which jogs along nicely creating a fun up-beat style. It works really well with a guitar driving the rhythm throughout the piece.

Originally written in E to be sung by a contemporary tenor singer, we have taken it down a tone to D to make it slightly more accessible to most singers – especially those of the female variety! Feel free to jack it up higher if you have someone with the appropriate voice.

The theme is Christmas, and the song talks about the age-old chestnut 'what is Christmas really about?' But it's done in a fun, quirky way, with verse 1 talking about a girl who has gone to watch her son in his nativity play, worrying about what she's going to buy him for Christmas and how she's going to pay for it. In verse 2 she has to endure comments from the people in the seat next to hers about their daughter, who is also in the play and who is a 'natural for her age'!

The song is written as if Jesus is singing it as he observes the frenzied seasonal activities of this world, and this is illustrated in the chorus, where the words state: 'Well I'm thinking 'bout Christmas and you know what I see Is that you're burying me beneath the Christmas tree And I need to know if you've forgotten my name and the reason why I came.'

Verse 3 talks about the department-store Santa. Finally, verse 4 is designed to be sung far more simply and quietly when it says, 'there I am, in the cradle with no lines to say at all and it makes me think of the stable when you thought of me as more than a doll'.

The song picks up again in tempo and volume with the final refrain of two choruses.

The Nativity Play

Shuffle ♩ = 124 (♫ = ♪ ³♪)

1. There's a

girl,　a sec - re - ta - ry,＿　and she's watch-ing a na - ti - vi - ty play,
(2.) front . . .
(3.) Santa . . .
(4.) there . . .

＿　and she　could have been　get-ting some ov - - er - time,　but she

pro-mised her son＿ she would stay,＿　and she's think-ing of　what she can buy

＿ him,＿　though she's　not　got　the mon - ey　to　spend＿

Verse 1
There's a girl, a secretary, and she's watching a nativity play,
and she could have been getting some overtime,
    but she promised her son she would stay,
and she's thinking of what she can buy him,
    though she's not got the money to spend
and though she could have been working tonight she really had to attend.

Verse 2
And at the front I can see a family whose daughter is up on the stage,
and they keep on telling their neighbours that she's a natural for her age,
and I know that they're secretly laughing when the other kids forget their
    lines,
and the prize for tonight's best actress is what's on their minds.

Chorus
Well I'm thinking 'bout Christmas, and you know what I see
is that you're burying me beneath the Christmas tree.
And I need to know if you've forgotten my name and the reason why I came,
the reason why I came.

Verse 3
And Santa Claus is in the staff room with the *Sunday Sport* in his hand,
and he's wishing he could be with the girl on page three
    in the sun and the sea and the sand,
but then he thinks of the money he's getting and he's hoping that his belly
    won't fall,
So he wipes the ash off his beard as he makes his way to the hall.

Chorus

Verse 4
And there I am in the cradle with no lines to say at all
And it makes me think of the stable where you thought of me as more than a
    doll
And I'm calling you as your Master and I'm calling you as your King
And I wanna be with you this Christmas so come on and invite me in.

Chorus

We Will Remember Them

Words and music by Mandy Watsham

This song is a ballad that builds.

It is ideal for a Remembrance Sunday event or themes talking about war or sacrifice.

The intro is loosely based on Reveille and is designed to be played freely and poignantly. Much of the song refers to the First World War, when thousands of young men went off on a great 'adventure' from which they never returned.

The chorus is referring back to Ivor Novello's song 'We'll Gather Lilacs', which was written during the Second World War. This followed on from his huge hit during the First World War, 'Keep the Home Fires Burning'. Both were great morale-boosters to the people back home, with lines such as 'We'll gather lilacs in the spring again and walk together down an English lane, until our hearts have learned to sing again, when you come home once more.'

Verse 3 could really be referring to any war from a soldier's perspective: 'miles from home in a war-torn hell where nothing now seems real'.

The message of the song is really about the futility of war, and that we who now live in freedom should remember those who gave everything in the line of duty and honour.

This piece was written to immediately follow the sketch 'Remembrance Day', also in this book, which adds to the poignant underlying message of the drama.

We Will Remember Them

Ballad, poignant ♩ = 56

VERSE

1. As the sun sets on an-oth-er day___ we will not let them
2. Bright, young, . . .
3. Games that . . .

fade___ a - way,___ and as morn-ing dawn streaks the___ skies

their sac - ri - fice_____ will ne-ver, ne - ver die.___

1.

2.3.

- mongst ten thou-sand dead._____

BRIDGE

We will re -

a tempo

- mem-ber what they gave,_ that led them to an ear - ly grave and

Verse 1
As the sun sets on another day
we will not let them fade away,
and as morning dawn streaks the skies
their sacrifice will never, never die.

Verse 2
Bright, young, full of life, their mothers' pride and joy,
standing tall and proud, these khaki soldier boys.
All the dreams they had for what would lie ahead
lay in fragments in the blood-soaked ground
        amongst ten thousand dead.

Bridge
We will remember what they gave,
that led them to an early grave and ...

Chorus
Now our hearts can sing again
as we stroll down our English lanes,
and those who now will not grow old
live on in memories and what we're told.
This legacy they left they gave together
is now our inheritance forever.

Verse 3
Games that once gave joy as through the woods they ran
Now meant life or death as boy turned into man
Home life never had such a strong appeal
When you're living in a war-torn hell and nothing now seems real.

Bridge

Chorus

Play out

The Christmas Ox

Alison Wright

This monologue features a young person at drama school who has a holiday job playing the Christmas Grotto ox in the local department store.

Nikki had high hopes for a job playing a Christmas fairy or elf at Selfridge's, at the very least. However, most of the good roles had gone, and as she is not the most dainty person the only role she was offered was that of the ox.

Her job is to hand out leaflets to potential clients and usher them into the Grotto. She is clearly unhappy throughout the piece as she attempts to interact with shoppers and spectacularly fails to attract their attention. When she is not attempting this, the rest of the time she speaks directly to the audience; this is when we realise that she really doesn't like children at all!

👩	👨	🕐
1	0	3 minutes

Other themes

Fitting in, children, self-esteem

Characters

NIKKI: A stereotypical stage school character, possibly a simple loud-mouthed northern lass

Costumes

Ridiculous ox outfit

All you need

❏   Handfuls of leaflets

[NIKKI enters, desperately trying to look excited, but can't hide the fact that she is uncomfortable, nervous and unconvincing.]

NIKKI: Hello, everybody. Merry Christmas and welcome to Santa's Grotto.

(to passing shopper and trying to thrust a leaflet in their hand) Hello, would you like to …? *(she tails off as they obviously walk past)*

Well, here I am again. Another day in the office. That's £31,000 spent on fees at RADA, only to look forward to my nine-to-five dressed as Santa's little helper.

At first I thought it was my big break. I mean, a part in Santa's Grotto at Harrods isn't half bad. But my luck wouldn't stretch to such heights!

First, I was demoted from Harrods to the Wolverhampton Woolies' Winter Wonderland, only to be told that I was too feminine to play Santa and yet too masculine to play Mrs Santa! After seeing me in my elf costume the boss told me my thighs were too chunky for the tunic and, deciding it best not to scare the children, they thought it was safest to keep my trunks covered. The position of Rudolph was already filled, so they created a new role for me. So here I am – the Christmas ox! *(makes ox-like sound, then quotes from company job description with more than a little sarcasm)* 'Here to create a cosy Christmas atmosphere and ever present to be patted, petted and prodded by the lovely kiddies.'

(trying again with another shopper) Hello! Would you like to …?

(and another shopper) You there, would you like to …?

The worst thing about this job is not the costume; it's not the eight hours of torturing embarrassment I have to face on a daily basis; it's not even the humiliating regular grunting noises I have to make. It's the kids. The job would be OK if I wasn't terrified of them! It's just that they're so small it seems unnatural. Take away the children, and I'm happy spending all day grunting away, dressed as something that seems to resemble a life-sized – well, never mind what. If I could just grunt away in a corner, bringing Christmas cheer to all, then my life would be perfectly happy.

(trying to thrust another leaflet in the hand of an unsuspecting passing shopper) Hello, would you like to ...?

(with resolve) I'm going to have to be braver if I want to get anywhere in this job. And I've heard Rudolph is leaving at the end of the week, so there may be a promotion in the offing. I've just got to be brave.

(to passing shopper with forced cheerfulness in voice) Merry Christmas! Would you and your lovely little girl like to ...? Would you ...? *(incredulous)* Would you really? Great, come on then *(gesturing behind)*, it's just through here ... Hey, what are you laughing at? *(getting upset)* Don't laugh at me, please. Please, just go through ... NO, it's not my real nose, and NO, THIS IS NOT PADDING!

Oh, I hate this job. I hate children and I hate Christmas.

[Blackout]

'Er Indoors

Nicki Matthews

This is a monologue from the perspective of someone who had first-hand experience of the events on the first Good Friday. At the beginning of the sketch we are not sure who we are listening to, but as time goes on we realise it is the wife of Pontius Pilate, the man who had Jesus put to death.

Based on the Gospel recordings of those three days, this sketch gives us an insight into what it was like for those closely involved in the action. It shows us what an impact Jesus had on the people around him at that time, and gives us some background to Pilate and how he struggled with the trials and verdicts he had to reach on behalf of the people.

Obviously best suited to Eastertime, this sketch can be used to great effect to bring the facts of the crucifixion and resurrection to those who would not usually read them in the Bible.

It also manages to bring a touch of humour to the story, based on the biblical recording that Pilate's wife did warn him about his decision, but 'he never listens'!

👩	👨	🕐
1	0	3 minutes

Other themes

Wanting to be popular, relationships

Characters

MRS PILATE: In her thirties to forties, ambitious for her husband but thinks she knows better than him. A little bit interfering.

Costumes

Simple black dress

All you need

❏   No props needed

MRS PILATE: I told him not to do it. I've had a dream, I said – a very vivid dream, I said. Don't have anything to do with that man, I said. But did he listen? Of course he didn't! Does he ever? He's a man – do I even need to ask the question?

Huh, it's a joke that women are the weaker sex! He didn't exactly hold on to the courage of his convictions for long, did he? It didn't take the Sannies long to change his mind at six in the morning, did it? What a rude awakening! A crowd of people banging on your door demanding blood at that time in the morning!

I mean, he told me himself he thought the chap was innocent. Couldn't find anything in any of their reports that he could make stick. Three times he declared the bloke not guilty. Three times! There wasn't a shred of evidence against him! And still they wanted him to sign off the sentence of death.

I thought it was bad enough when he agreed to the flogging. I mean, what had the poor chap done to deserve it? From what I could hear, through the glass on the other side of the wall, they were accusing him of the three Ts: tax evasion, treason and terrorism. I mean – terrorism! I've never seen anyone less like a terrorist in all my life! And anyway, they had nothing to back it up. That's why they resorted to bribery.

I mean, I know Pilate's had a tough time since he took over the governorship of this province. The Jewish people just didn't take to him. I don't know why. Maybe he was a bit rude about some of their traditions – but there was no need for a full-scale riot. I couldn't sleep for weeks after that. And when news got back to head office, they pulled him in and gave him a verbal warning. Then the rabble threatened to lodge a formal complaint with the PM – and, well, that was enough to turn him to drink. The thought of being sacked and called back to Rome – well, it was more than the poor man could bear. He's got his whole career mapped out, you know. Governor by 30, PM by 40 and retirement in a cosy bungalow on the coast by 50. So, he succumbed to the pressure.

He must have known it was a frame-up. I mean, why else would they come to him and the government they obviously hated and ask for the death of one of their own people?

He knew what was right, but he had to keep the peace – it was more than his job's worth – and that just blurred his vision. He can't stand not being popular, bless him, so he made his choice.

But I told him it was the wrong choice – I've been telling him most of the weekend and he's just stuck his head in the sand and refused to listen. He knows I'm right: he just doesn't want to admit it.

I'm glad he let them bury him, though. That was a nice touch. I think they needed to grieve for him properly, and it gave him confirmation that he was actually dead – not that there should have been any doubt, but what with all the media coverage it was good to make one hundred per cent sure.

That's why I can't understand all the kerfuffle this morning. Another early morning call – I thought the door really was going to cave in this time, what with all the banging and shouting and the paparazzi absolutely swarming around the front garden.

And before I even had one arm in the sleeve of my dressing gown, he had his trousers on and was out of the door without so much as a by-your-leave.

I haven't seen him since, and his dinner's completely ruined. I can't imagine what's happened that's so important he'd miss his roast beef and Yorkshires, but it's bound to be something to do with Friday's shenanigans.

I knew he should have listened to me.

[Blackout]

Christmas in Captivity

Adapted by David Robinson from Taken on Trust

This is a simple but very powerful monologue, based on Terry Waite's description of his third Christmas as a hostage in Beirut. The description has been adapted from *Taken on Trust: Recollections from Captivity* (Hodder & Stoughton, 1993)

Where possible, this should be performed on an almost dark stage, save for the light of one small candle, to create a feeling of solitude for the actor on stage. The text begins on Christmas Eve, when Terry should be enjoying celebrations with his friends and family. In reality, he will 'celebrate' with a sandwich and the four walls of the tiny cell in which he has been incarcerated for three years. Everything familiar has been taken away from him except a small prayer book. Saving a small piece from his sandwich and making a cross from an old tissue, Terry spends Christmas Eve taking communion. The familiar symbols remind him of the sacrifice Jesus made, and he determines not to feel pity for himself.

This moving scene illustrates so clearly that, even when everything familiar is taken away, the one thing that remains constant is God's faithfulness; we can rely on him even in times of great uncertainty.

NB: If possible, follow this monologue with the song 'Great is Thy Faithfulness', found earlier in this book. The introduction should begin as soon as Terry has uttered his last words.

♀	♂	🕐
0	1	3 minutes

Other themes

Christmas, war

Characters

TERRY WAITE: Prisoner in Beirut, stooped and tired

Costumes

Black trousers and black top, bare feet

All you need

❑ One candle, on a tall stand or table so as to be seen
❑ Small prayer book
❑ Cross made out of a tissue (inside the prayer book)
❑ Piece of bread (inside the prayer book)

[The stage is almost dark, with just the light of the candle. This monologue is more effective if the paragraphs are separated by poignant pauses.]

TERRY: Can you tell me the date, please? The date? Thank you. The 24th of December. Christmas Eve. I can remember being here twelve months ago, celebrating my second Christmas in captivity. Celebrating! Three years! Three years …

It's cold tonight. Normally I sit cross-legged by my candle, wrapped in a blanket like some kind of Indian tailor.

Three years! I remember what I used to say to the families of the other hostages. Three years – it's make or break time, you know. Make or break. That's me now.

Three years without feeling the wind or the rain or the sun. Three years without a decent conversation with anybody. *(his voice is getting louder)* Three years in chains! How long can this go on?

It must be nearly Christmas Day.

I try not to think about my family and friends back home, celebrating. It hurts too much.

Two thousand years ago, not many miles from here, Jesus was born, a man of sorrows. Such grief, such pain. *(louder and more determined)* I will not feel pity for myself.

I have decided to celebrate Christmas with communion. I have a candle, a little prayer book, I kept back a tiny piece of bread from my sandwich, and I've made a little cross from a tissue I found.

[he opens his prayer book]

John's Gospel says, 'The light will shine in the darkness and we beheld his glory, full of grace and full of truth.' Jesus took the bread and broke it and said, 'This is my body. It's broken for you. Do this in remembrance of me.'

May his light shine in my darkness.

Star of the Show

Nicki Matthews and Mandy Watsham

This duologue features two five-year-olds discussing who is the most important character in the school nativity play.

Emily is playing Gabriel, and is clearly a confident little girl who firmly believes that her character, as the one who brings the message to the world, is definitely the most important character.

Josh, on the other hand, is playing Joseph, and clearly in his family the father is most important person.

This is a comical look at children's perception of the nativity story, but it perhaps highlights how many people miss the point of the central character at Christmas.

NB: If only females are available, you could replace Joseph with Mary. Alternative dialogue appears in italics where necessary.

👩	👨	🕐
1*	1*	4 minutes

* or 2 of each if you change the lead characters

Other themes

Childhood, self-obsession, family relationships

Characters

EMILY:	Bossy little girl playing Gabriel, used to being listened to and to people doing what she says!
JOSH:	Little boy playing Joseph, rather in awe of Emily but not willing to be totally walked over
JENNIFER:	Playing Mary

Costumes

EMILY:	Hair in bunches, white dress and halo
JOSH:	Dressing gown, sandals
JENNIFER:	Blue smock and headdress

All you need

❏   Doll representing Jesus

EMILY: *(addressing audience proudly)* We're doing a nativity play

JOSH: *(addressing audience equally proudly)* Yeah – it's a Christmas nativity play. *(cradling Jesus in arms)*

EMILY: Yeah, and guess what I am. Bet you can't!

JOSH: I can.

EMILY: Shut up! *(to audience, speaking slowly and deliberately)* I'm the Angel Gabriel. Miss Stoke said she chose me because Gabriel was the one what told everybody what to do and that suited me.

JOSH: You can say that again!

EMILY: And that makes me the most important person in the whole play!

JOSH: I don't agree, actually!

EMILY: Really?

JOSH: Well, no, because I'm the baby's father and the father is always the most important person.

JENNIFER: *Well, no, 'cos I think my Joseph is the most important person 'cos he's the father and the Daddy is always the most important.*

EMILY: Not in my house. My mummy says my daddy's a complete waste of space – what did she call him this morning? Oh yes, a silly so …

JOSH: *(quickly interrupting)* So, what about Mary?

EMILY: Oh no, she's not important at all – all she's interested in is buying CDs from HMV or Virgin or some other record shop. I think the innkeeper's quite important, though. *(all coy)* He's my boyfriend *(waves to off stage)*.

JOSH: No, he's not! Just 'cos he sat next to you at lunch and pulled your bunches doesn't mean he loves you. *(Jesus doll now being held by one hand instead of carefully cradled)*

EMILY: Does!

JOSH: Doesn't!

EMILY: Does!

JOSH: Doesn't! Anyway, he's stupid – he can't even get his lines right. He keeps telling me to try the breakfast and bed down the road!

EMILY: Well, I think that's very helpful, actually!

JOSH: No, it's not. They won't have any room either, will they? It's Christmas, stupid!

EMILY: So what about the shepherds?

JOSH: They can't be important. They were washing their socks when all the good stuff was going on. The kings were, though. They were really, really rich. Richer than anyone in the whole wide world. Even richer than Charlotte Church!

EMILY: No way! How do you know?

JOSH: Well, they bought really expensive presents for the baby.

EMILY: What, like a computer or a bike?

JOSH: No, nothing like that. I don't think there was a Toys 'R' Us in their town. No, they bought gold …

EMILY: *(in wonder)* Gold what?

JOSH: Um *(trying to impress)* gold stars, I think … *(hurrying on)* and merrr …

EMILY: More?

JOSH: No, merrr.

EMILY: What's merrr?

JOSH: I think it's like Vaseline, stinky stuff, but I'm not sure … and something else, 'cept I can't remember what.

EMILY: I know – it was a Frankenstein!

JOSH: Oh yes – a Frankenstein!

EMILY: 'Cept I think that was a bit mean, 'cos the baby was only little and he would have been scared and cried all night.

JOSH: But he did have his ass.

EMILY: *(shocked)* Joshua – don't be so rude! I'm telling of you. Miss Stoke, Miss Stoke … Joshua said a rude word …

JOSH: What are you talking about? He had an ox and an ass in the stable with him, looking after him. He was sleeping in their food bowl, you know! *(doll Jesus being dangled by one leg!)*

EMILY: Err yuk! That's horrible!

JOSH: Now, King Harold, he was really important and really nasty, like – who's that really horrid scary man on the news?

EMILY: Sadman Huslain.

JOSH: No, no, the other one who Daddy says is a thief and a liar – oh, I know, Phony Blair.

EMILY: Yes, Harold was a really bad man. He stabbed all the baby boys in the eye with an arrow and then he poisoned them with mouldy Kit-Kats.

JOSH: Yuk, I don't like Kit-Kats.

EMILY: No neither do I. I like jelly babies.

JOSH: Babies *(remembers baby in his hand and carefully cradles it again)* – what about the baby in the food bowl? He must be quite important.

EMILY: Why?

JOSH: Well, 'cos all the others wouldn't have bothered visiting him, would they?

EMILY: I suppose not.

JOSH: In fact, it says in the book where Miss Stoke got this story from that he was the Son of God. 'Today in the town of David a Saviour has been born, he is Christ the Lord.' *(reading the lines as if learnt by rote)*

EMILY: So, then, if that's the case and this baby is going to be the Saviour of the world – then whoever came to tell everyone about him would have to be really important, wouldn't they?

JOSH: I suppose so.

EMILY: So I was right. I am the most important person in the whole show! Come and help me polish my halo please, Joseph.

[Fade out]

Remembrance Day?

Nicki Matthews and Mandy Watsham

The action for this sketch takes place during the two-minute silence on Remembrance Sunday, probably at a parade.

It features four people and their memories of four different wars – the Great War, the Second World War, the Falklands War and a recent conflict such as the Bosnian War. It shows how these wars have had a long-lasting effect on their lives and the lives of those close to them.

The four characters stand in a haphazard line across the stage, and the dialogue is actually their innermost thoughts. It can therefore either be recited by the characters on stage, or voices back-stage can read the lines in order to portray that the characters are merely thinking. A spotlight on the face of each person at the appropriate time would be most effective, particularly if the voice is coming from off-stage.

At the end of each character's dialogue, the first line from the next character overlaps with the same words. The underlying feelings seem to be that although they are there to remember those who sacrificed their lives in the wars, all they really want to do is forget the wars and move on.

NB: The person reading the announcements off-stage could potentially be the voices for Stan and Luke (assuming he has a talent for different voices/accents). You could then use one female for the two ladies' voices (assuming the same as above).

👩	👨	🕐
2	3	4 minutes

Other themes

Futility of war

Characters

DORIS:	Elderly lady – probably sitting – born in 1915 and remembering the loss of her father in the First World War
STAN:	World War II veteran of the Battle of Britain, standing tall but with a stick
HELEN:	Wife of a soldier who fought in the Falklands War; about 40
LUKE:	Soldier in his twenties who has just returned from the Balkans
VOICE:	Preferably male, to announce the two-minute silence

Costumes

DORIS:	Coat, hat and scarf with rug over her knees
STAN:	Dark suit and tie with medal
HELEN:	Dress and coat
LUKE:	Combat uniform or something to indicate he is a soldier

All you need

❑ Chair for Doris
❑ Sound effect: clock chiming 11 a.m.

[All four characters are on stage – not in a line, but haphazardly. The clock chimes 11 a.m.]

VOICE: At the eleventh hour of the eleventh day of the eleventh month … They shall grow not old as we that are left grow old. Age shall not weary them, nor the years condemn.

DORIS: I never knew my father, but I do know what a brave and courageous man he was. I was born just three weeks before my mother received the telegram. He'd been away only two months and was killed twelve days after arriving at the trenches. I could never understand why my mother used to cry on 18 March every year, but as I got older and learnt of the total futility of those young men going off to the front line – heads held high, proud to be defending their country, unaware of the horrors awaiting them – I began to comprehend some of the despair and sorrow that became so much a part of her. Now, I never miss this opportunity to come and honour the memory of his life, and the lives of all his comrades on the battlefields of France. Sadly, Mother never remarried, even though she was still so young. The war changed our lives for ever …

STAN: *(starting to speak as* DORIS *starts her last line, therefore speaking the same line together)* The war changed our lives for ever. I was training to be a pilot in 1939, so I was one of the first to sign up to the RAF. I lived to fly and fell in love with the Spitfire the moment I clapped eyes on it. It was 14 October 1940 when my life changed in an instant. I was caught from behind by a Messerschmitt 109, somewhere over West Sussex. A shell exploded in the cockpit, and from that moment it felt as if my whole body was on fire. The intense pain overwhelmed me. Somehow I managed to bale out and was picked up by a farmer who got me to hospital. I lost all the sight in my left eye and most in the right on that day, and the wounds in my leg and chest were very slow to heal. I didn't think I'd make it to my wedding, scheduled for 14 December, but we were married on time, even though I'm sad to say I couldn't see her wedding dress or her sunny smile. Margaret became my wife and my nurse on that day – I came back from war a different man …

HELEN: *(starting to speak as STAN starts his last line, therefore speaking the same line together)* … came back from war a different man. Completely changed. When he left for Port Stanley he was a loving husband and father, but he came back bitter and twisted. He always makes us come to this parade. Every year without fail. He says, 'It's important for us to remember those who gave their lives for their country.' I suppose he's right, but I'm sure it's not been good for the children. They've grown up with a father more preoccupied with the Falklands than them. I know it's difficult for him to forget some of the things he saw. And I know it hit him really hard to lose his best friend at Goose Green like that. I'd do anything to try and help him, but he won't let me. I've been trying for nearly 18 years, but the sights and sounds of the war still haunt …

LUKE: *(starting to speak as HELEN starts her last line, therefore speaking the same line together)* … the sights and sounds of the war still haunt me when I close my eyes at night. We were supposed to be there to keep the peace. Peace! What a joke! I don't think I witnessed a minute of peace the whole time I was there. A once peaceful country – not that far from our own – torn apart by hate and anger. I can still hear the heart-rending sobs of the women whose husbands and sons had been taken. Still remember the wails of the babies who were hungry and didn't understand why there wasn't any food. Still sense the fear and disgust in the hearts of the young girls who will never trust a man again. And I can still see the look in the eyes of men who had grown up together but who now hated each other enough to kill.

Here we are today to remember the wars – but truly …

ALL: I just want to forget.

VOICE: At the going down of the sun and in the morning, we will remember them.

ALL: We will remember them.

The Night before Christmas

Tim Goodwright

This comical sketch is very loosely based on the BBC TV sitcom *The Royle Family*.

It is Christmas Eve. The Crownes, a typical family, are celebrating the festive season. With bickering between siblings, strained relationships and an aversion to attending church if it disturbs the Christmas TV, most families can relate to the scene!

Mr Crowne, who we assume does not usually attend church on a regular basis, is insistent that the whole family attends midnight mass together. This is to the chagrin of his two teenage children, who are in the middle of watching a film, and his wife, whose feet are aching.

The perception of church seen by the characters in this sketch sadly echoes around the country, and is perhaps a sad reminder of why our churches are in decline.

👩	👨	⏱
2	2	5 minutes

Other themes

Family life

Characters

JOHN:	Middle-aged, 'head of the household' type, determined his family *will* enjoy Christmas together
PAM:	Rather meek wife and mother, wanting to please everybody
DARREN:	Moody teenager, 16 to 19 years old
JANE:	Mature younger sister, 13 to 15 years old

Costumes

JOHN:	Slacks and cardigan with slippers
PAM:	Skirt and blouse with slippers
DARREN:	Jeans and t-shirt
JANE:	Jeans and jumper

All you need

❏ Settee and chair (à la *Royle Family*)
❏ Telephone
❏ Sound effect: telephone ringing
❏ Remote control

[The Crowne family are sitting watching television. JOHN is in the chair, PAM and JANE are on the sofa, DARREN is lounging on the floor. As the scene opens the telephone is ringing but nobody moves. Eventually JOHN, the father, gets up and answers it.]

JOHN: I'll get it, then shall I? Hello? Hello? *(rolling his eyes)* Rita, how are you? Of course it's me!

[PAM indicates from the sofa that she does not want to speak to her.]

Yes, Pammy is fine *(beckoning her to the phone)* – and the kids *(they indicate the same)* … How about you? And Brian? Still mixing concrete, then? Good! Oh, you know what it's like – work, work, work … *(he is obviously trying to be very nice)* No, we don't really get to see Dad that often nowadays – well, he just seems to be so happy at the home! He's been making a laundry basket, would you believe? I know, I know! You just can't keep a good man down! *(sighing and looking at his watch)* Ah dear – yes, yes, and a happy Christmas to you as well! And a Happy New Year – I said Happy New Year! Have a good one! All right, you take care now. Goodbye! Goodbye! *(he hangs up)*

Well, that's the annual phone call done with.

DARREN: Shut up, Dad, I'm trying to watch the telly!

JOHN: And a fat lot of help you were!

PAM: Darren, don't talk to your father like that. I never know what to say – she's your sister, anyway.

JOHN: That's not the point, Pam – what I was looking for was a little bit of support. Right, come along, family, it's nearly time. *(sits down again in the armchair)*

JANE: Oh, Dad, do we have to?

JOHN: Yes, we do. It's all part of the tradition of this family – goodness knows there isn't much. We are going to midnight mass.

DARREN: But, Dad, this doesn't finish until ten to twelve.

JOHN: Well, video it then.

DARREN: But I'm already videoing Sky One.

PAM: Darren, did you record that Frank Sinatra thing on BBC2 for me?

DARREN: No.

PAM: Why not?

DARREN: Because the *Star Trek* trilogy was on in widescreen.

PAM: Anyone would think it was your machine! Tell him, John.

JANE: He never lets anybody else use that video.

JOHN: Darren, do as your mother says. Jane, stop stirring. *(pause; then, looking at the TV)* Who is he?

PAM: His brother was the one that was murdered at the train station, and it's his girlfriend that was in the restaurant.

JOHN: So why is he carrying the nappies?

JANE: So he doesn't look suspicious when he goes to the party …

JOHN: *(working it out and struggling)* Well, I'm confused – I don't know about anyone else!

DARREN: Shhhhh!

PAM: *(pointedly)* Jane, could you massage my feet for me please? *(she puts her legs across JANE on the sofa)*

JANE: Are your feet hurting you still, Mum?

PAM: I'm in absolute agony.

JOHN: *(twigging)* Hey, now don't start that way with me because it won't work.

JANE: But, Dad, you can't seriously expect Mum to go to church when her feet are hurting so much.

JOHN: And I suppose you're willing to stay behind and look after her?

JANE: Oh yes. I'd be delighted.

DARREN: *(copying her)* 'Oh yes. I'd be delighted.' I bet you would.

JANE: Shut up, Darren.

JOHN: We're all going to church and that's the end of it, feet or no feet.

DARREN: Why?

JOHN: Because I say so.

DARREN: But it's so boring.

JANE: And cold.

PAM: *(the peacemaker)* Look, if the kids don't want to go, how about just you and me going together, eh?

JOHN: Because Christmas is a time for families to suffer together – over-eating, relatives and church.

DARREN: What's the point of going to church anyway?

PAM: *(nicely)* It's Jesus's birthday.

DARREN: So what?

JANE: You are so thick, Darren.

DARREN: No, I'm not. I just can't see the point of celebrating some bloke's birthday I'm not interested in.

JANE: Good! You won't mind if we don't celebrate yours, then?

[DARREN hits her round the head.]

PAM: Stop it, the pair of you. I'm not going to have all this fighting at Christmas.

DARREN: But we have fighting for the rest of the year – a sister is for life, not just for Christmas.

JANE: Ha ha! Very funny.

JOHN: What's everybody got against going to church for midnight mass all of a sudden?

DARREN: It's boring.

JANE: And cold.

JOHN: Apart from cold and boring, it's the only 45 minutes I ask you to spend in church a year.

DARREN: *(folding his arms)* Auntie Jill got married this year so I've already done my time in church this year.

JANE:	*(mockingly)* And who could ever forget you passing out at the reception after two glasses of champagne?
DARREN:	It must have been fortified champagne.
JOHN:	We are going to midnight mass. Do you seriously want to spoil Christmas Day by going in the morning?
JANE:	But we don't go any other day of the year, yet we have to make this great big show of it on Christmas Eve.
DARREN:	*(joining in)* That's right. We don't even believe in all that religious stuff for the rest of the year.
PAM:	What a thing to say! We've brought you up on good Christian principles in this house, young man. You don't have to go to church every week to live a good life.
JOHN:	Thank you, Pammy – you two listen to your mother.

[Pause; they watch the TV.]

	Why did he have to take nappies? I don't see why he didn't take a bottle to the party like everyone else ...
JANE:	It's a baby shower, Dad.
JOHN:	I don't care how big it is! *(laughs)* I don't care how big it is ... Baby shower, big shower – get it? Did you get it, Darren?
DARREN:	*(rolling his eyes)* Yes, Dad – and yes, I did get a shower this morning just before anyone says anything.
JANE:	You could have fooled me!
PAM:	Pack it in, you two.
JOHN:	Right, that does it! *(stands up and turns off the TV)*
PAM:	John!
JOHN:	You two, up and out – same for you, Pam. We are going to midnight mass and that's the end of it.

[They reluctantly get up and make their way off.]

JANE: Our father who art annoying, 'Bah humbug' is thy name …

PAM: That's enough out of you, young lady.

DARREN: *(sarcastically)* Ho, ho, ho – Merry Christmas, everyone.

JOHN: *(calling off)* Go and get your coats on – I'll see you at the car.
                 *(turns on the TV again and watches standing up – remote in
                 hand)* I still think nappies were the wrong decision myself. Still
                 it's *The Sound of Music* tomorrow. I wonder if I'll have as much
                 trouble getting them to watch the Queen at three o'clock …

[PAM enters with her coat.]

PAM: Have you turned off the … JOHN! Honestly! I'll be in the car.
                 (exits angrily)

JOHN: *(puts the remote control on the chair and shakes his fist at the
                 heavens)* I HOPE YOU APPRECIATE THIS!

[He exits.]

If you are interested in obtaining a CD of the songs featured in this book please contact us at the address below for further details.

Chrysalis
78 The Broadway
Chesham
Bucks
HP5 1EG

You might also be interested in our previous recordings, *Cracking the Church Cocoon* and *Soulmates*, both available on CD or cassette.